I came that they may have life,
and have it abundantly.

———

JOHN 10:10

Lovingly dedicated to
the one person who taught me most
about the power of Hope,
about trusting completely in God,
and about never giving up:
My Husband

Contents

Foreword

Our Holy Father, Pope John Paul II, increasingly expresses concern about modern society's embrace of "The Culture of Death." Especially in the United States today abortion on demand, suicide, and euthanasia advocacy abound.

If this Culture of Death seems un-Christian—it is! Neither the Good Shepherd nor the Good Samaritan bore the equivalent of a canister of carbon monoxide or deliberate overdose to lost sheep or sufferer left by the wayside.

Reviewing *The Healing Power of Hope*, one intuits that it is particularly timely and that it will achieve classic status as a beacon in the evident growing darkness. Mary Drahos' *oeuvre* is pure gold refined in the crucible of a human life lived with tenacity, courage, and dedication.

For the afflicted mentally, physically, and spiritually, and those who, in love or duty, care for or about them, *The Healing Power of Hope* sings. It is about the power of powerlessness, about pain and joy, purpose and commitment, about suffering and surcease, caliper and key—spirituality and inner peace. Selected Scriptural quotations, prose, and prayer sparkle like jewels across the text.

All seeking meaning in human life and the crosses indigenous thereto will discover a rich treasure here.

Dr. Joseph R. Stanton, M.D.

Author's Preface

Suffering can be a very enigmatic experience. It envelops every person alive at one time or another, yet it is as intense or as varied as people are themselves. It is poorly understood and, for the most part, utterly detested. Even many Christians have a misconstrued understanding of suffering and why a loving God allows it. Too often they dismiss the powerful theological virtue of *hope*. The end result is more suffering.

But who wants to suffer? Nobody who is sane. Even saints rejected suffering for its own sake. Suffering *per se* does not ennoble us. It does not make us reach out to others. It cultivates neither feelings of compassion nor spurts of empathy. In short, pain and suffering are things we do our utmost to resist because we sense something inherently evil and negative when our wholeness is challenged. It seems to sap our personhood, to make us do and say and think things which we generally abhor.

Yet there's the human condition, all varieties and degrees of serious pain or hurt: the lightning-like shock of a fall on the ski slope; the unremitting agony of a chronic or incurable disease; the grinding vacuum of constant rejection; the unbelievable loneliness of old age; the monumental struggle of the mentally and physically disabled to "keep on keeping on." In a sense, all are suspended in dynamic equilibrium, like Alice in Wonder land.

For all those who experience suffering, there are not only different thresholds of pain but, more importantly, different expectations of both healing and hopelessness. Feelings range from something like, "I'll *just die* if this awful bursitis doesn't go away!" to "Well, the chemotherapy won't be a picnic. But, Lord, it may be your tool for healing my cancer, I'll pray and stick with it."

There appear to be various approaches when it comes to handling most kinds of suffering. Initially, we reject it (like reaching for aspirin as a headache builds momentum). Next, when the prognosis is specific and we fully anticipate a recovery, we resign ourselves to the temporary discomfort and inconvenience (like coping with a clumsy cast when we have broken a leg).

Should our problem present a more static pathology, with no real hope of healing, we may find ourselves dealing with it on a highly emotional level. As we become progressively more debilitated, it is as though the sword of Damocles were suspended over our heads. This thing neither kills us nor promises any kind of lasting remission.

Finally, as we inevitably age and there is cellular breakdown in our bodies, there is often spiritual and psychological warfare within. We may make ludicrous attempts to deny the obvious and grasp for whatever illusive fountain of youth presents itself. All the while, however, we harbor a secret terror of death.

Redemptive Suffering

In the final analysis, whatever the suffering, we come face to face with a choice. We can become so immersed in our condition that we are no longer a person with a problem. Instead we have allowed the problem to become our person. We can decide either to blame doctors, caregivers, loved ones, and some cruel fate—or we can transform it into powerful spiritual ammunition to bring incredible benefit for both ourselves and others. We can tap into "redemptive suffering."

To do so, however, we need to recognize the fact that many woes which are not necessarily life-threatening are self-induced, however unconsciously, and cannot be labeled "redemptive." It usually takes a good deal of objectivity and spiritual maturity to grasp this reality, but when we grasp it we are obliged to make the necessary changes. We do not glorify God, for instance, when we knowingly eat a food to which we are allergic. Perhaps even more important than a candid appraisal of our situation is to acknowledge the truth that God is the ultimate source of all healing. We may insist on top doctors and the best of medical care, but all this is futile unless it is in the Lord's will that there be restoration.

Most people would agree that suffering should not be merely accepted without seeking healing through medical means. But what about miraculous healing? Have we really become skeptics and closed our minds to "faith healing?" After all, when Jesus walked the face of our earth, he spent a great deal of time not only healing the sick himself but carefully instructing his followers to heal as well. As a matter of fact, with the subsequent outpouring of the Holy Spirit at Pentecost, the early Church exercised the charism of healing as a normal sign and wonder of the Good News of salvation.

If we truly believe that all things are possible with God, then we find no contradiction with getting medical and spiritual help simultaneously. There should be no either/or choice. After all, it is inconsequential to hear a doctor label something as an "inexplicable cure" rather than a "miracle." The hand of God is still in it. There is great truth in Tennyson's words that prayer effects "more things than this world dreams of."

So where, we might wonder, does this concept of redemptive suffering fit in? Is it just a religious cop-out when nothing seems to be working? What if we have gone for appropriate medical assistance and we have been praying, but still no apparent healing seems to be forthcoming?

To suffer redemptively means, quite simply, that we willingly suffer for the sake of the Kingdom. How can this be done? We begin by personally accepting the fact that earthly existence is flawed, it cannot be totally pain free. When suffering comes our way, therefore, we make a decided attempt to join our pain with all that Jesus deliberately endured out of love for us.

What happens then is something of a bonding—Jesus mysteriously right in us, suffering with us in our pain—as together we swell the Church's "spiritual treasury." Our suffering is not wasted. Of course, we still pray for and welcome his healing touch if and when and how he chooses, but at this moment we do not turn away like self-indulgent and spoiled children when he holds out his cross instead.

"Pray for one another, that you may be healed," we read in Scripture (Jas 5:16). Over the years I have prayed with and counseled many people, singly and in small groups. We who prayed were hardly problem-free ourselves, still we can attest to witnessing much healing in ourselves as we interceded for others. Sometimes Jesus healed in a spectacular way, like my own healing of legal blindness and getting a "totally normal" stomach after most was removed surgically for carcinoid tumors (gratefully noted in my book *To Touch the Hem of His Garment*).

There have been a great many more things, however, of which we were not healed and which we had to learn to offer up for the time being. Was it just some hiatus in God's healing schedule for us? Was he trying to teach us that only Heaven holds our perfect healing? In either case, we had to learn repeatedly one indispensable lesson when it comes to both suffering and healing: We humans must yield to God's will and not adamantly insist on our own.

This book is a composite of much prayer and surrender. It faces the same stark reality of suffering, fear, and despair that fellow human beings experience everywhere. In a personal way, however, it clarifies suffering for today's Christian—especially one who is ambiguous about the intrinsic value of each and every person whom God created.

The Healing Power of Hope

While suffering may be part of our common human lot, there is a striking difference between a sufferer who believes in an Almighty God and one with the worldly notion that "that's all there is." The difference lies in one word: HOPE. No matter how hopeless we may feel at times, as believers we realize the potential of eternal life, of trusting in things unseen or merely hoped for (see Hebrews 11:1).

The ultimate hope, of course, is to be released from the fear of death. As faithful followers of Jesus there should be no panic when our terminal state arrives. After all, in the eternal scheme of things, our lives do not end. They change. It is in the peace-filled acceptance of this spiritual truth—something inwardly arrived at long before our final moment—that we have real "death with dignity."

Along the road to this inevitable milestone, however, we are bombarded with the pressures of a post-Christian/Judaic society. It is often difficult to find concrete answers for coping with suffering in a spiritual way. Each chapter in this book, therefore, takes up the kind of emotional perceptions that might have plagued us or those we care for at one time or another. All these are explored and discussed candidly and informally—as though the reader and I were speaking across my kitchen table.

Each question is dealt with by 1) Setting Things Straight (We must first be aware of erroneous attitudes and misinformation.); 2) Looking to the Light (Did Jesus not say that no follower of his need walk in darkness?); and 3) Follow-Up Action (What is so often needed, but not received, are pragmatic suggestions for achieving a "spirituality of hope.")

These are contemporary, hands-on guidelines which can prove extremely useful during times of serious sickness, accidents, stress-induced depressions, aging, terminal illness, etc. Those with physical disabilities or a wide variety of handicaps may also gain a new insight on the power and life-enhancing value of hope. Along with love, Christians especially should manifest hope to the world.

This became very evident to me some years ago, when I was teaching a junior high school religious education class. One little boy in my class, Charlie, always came in late and slid into his chair with utmost reluctance. Afterwards he pulled himself up just as slowly, never speaking to anyone. Wanting to help, I coaxed Charlie into staying after class with me. I had hoped that a chat and a sugar donut would lift his spirits.

When the others had gone and Charlie was contentedly munching on his donut, I broached the subject. "Are you having any problems, Charlie? Maybe I can help."

"My ma has MS," he confided, "Y'know what that is?" I nodded.

"She's gonna be paralyzed and even get all blind," he went on with moist eyes. "The social worker, she made me move to my grandma's place. I don't see her much...."

That social worker had quite obviously based her evaluation on a worst-case scenario. It was ripping out Charlie's heart because even the hint of hope was smothered. Yet hope is what keeps us going. Through it, the Holy Spirit teaches us how to accept, how to cope, and how to adapt to a present situation while we accept inwardly that God will effect some kind of change in the future.

While the basic religious orientation of this book is Catholic, all Christians or anyone spiritually minded and open will find it optimistic and life-affirming. It was written to encourage, enlighten, and to rebut the deluge of books promoting suicide and euthanasia. It is an unabashed antidote to "creeping Kevorkianism." My sincere prayer is that readers will find here the divine power to choose life, no matter what, and to hope anyway!

About Perspectives...

All during childhood and early adolescence, whenever I was about to encounter someone with canes or crutches, I automatically crossed the street to avoid passing. Something about the individual left me extremely uncomfortable. There is nothing in my upbringing that would indicate a cause for such ostensible apprehension and I never mentioned it to anyone.

Years later, as a reporter for a daily newspaper, I once took a shortcut to the city room past a Tudor home elegantly withstanding commercial expansion. Around the corner, blocking my path, sat a large amiable gentleman in a wheelchair.

"I'm terribly sorry," I mumbled awkwardly, my heart racing.

"I'm not!" he laughed, stretching out a hand, "My name is Doctor Sykes. I teach philosophy over at the university. And you... breathless one...? Is it logical to presume that you also have a name?"

Thereupon ensued the first of many enjoyable conversations

over the next two years, whenever the weather and schedules allowed. I can still see his serene smile and his raised brows when I philosophized on my immature observations of life. In retrospect, I realize that not once did he allude to his disability.

There is no doubt that God placed him in my life to heal me of an unknown fear and to realize how Christ can be camouflaged in the hurting and broken ones among us. I am truly grateful for this "possibilities preview." What a loving Lord! I do not feel odd in my own wheelchair now, nor think that life is all but over and holds no joy. More importantly, I can empathize with people who avoid getting too close and understand when they act as if my disability were contagious.

As my professor friend might have observed, "They have a low 'hope quotient.' Actually, they have the greater handicap."

Hope Power and "The Old Flounder"

In the early 1960s Bill was a "lean and mean" ex-Marine when he confidently stepped up for the Salk vaccine, which was being publicly distributed. Like most people in the country, he welcomed this medical "breakthrough" preventing the dreaded polio. He was one of the extremely rare recipients, however, whose lives it would change forever. In what seemed like a cruel, ironic blow, he was afflicted with the crippling disease instead of receiving immunity against it.

Bill and his large Irish family—he had nine siblings—were totally stunned when he landed in the V.A. hospital's polio ward. He was overwhelmed by the painful feelings and questions that rushed at him from all directions. Who was he now? What would he do for the remainder of his life? How long was he expected to live? There was nothing left but to plead for help in prayer.

First Bill came to an assessment and "personal inventory." Except for his left arm, most of his body was totally immobile. However, looking around at fellow polio patients, he began to feel a bit fortunate. Many could not breathe for themselves and lay in iron lungs.

"That guy over there, he can only move one toe," he had informed Marilyn, his pretty, young physical therapist, nervous on her very first day as a medical professional. "Me? I've got one whole remarkable arm and, even if I can't use my legs, look at this useable head! After all, the real me isn't paralyzed, right?"

Bill Donnelly had been one of Marilyn's first patients. She realized there was a special quality about this man. Even before she met him, she had thought so: his name had leaped out at her from the patient assignment roster, though she couldn't think why. His extraordinary self-evaluation only confirmed her intuition. She would have to keep her wits about her with this patient. She must not seem flustered.

The next day they had another session together. She found herself laughing at his self-deprecating humor, like "Could have been worse. I could have stalled on the railroad tracks!" Determinedly, she turned her mind back to the routine of her job, trying to remember how it was that they were told in class to cover a patient's private areas before initiating any therapy. She fiddled with the sheets.

"Here, let me tell you what to do," Bill offered in the laughing voice of one well-versed in hospital routine. "Take the sheet and fold 'A' over 'B,' then pin at point 'C.' There! Comes with keen observation, wouldn't you say?"

"You're fantastic!" What she meant was *different*, pleasantly different from all the angry and uncooperative patients her therapist friends talked about. Day after day he would describe himself as "fine and dandy" or "dandy and fine" whenever she came. He even pronounced himself "perfect" at times.

One morning, in the middle of another session, Bill made a conspicuous show of flexing his muscles, which made her smile. Grinning back at her, he ran his hand over his slightly balding head and asked, "Tell the truth, Marilyn, isn't this the most capable left arm in the whole hospital? I'm a speed demon when they get me in a wheelchair and I take off down the hall!"

"As a matter of fact, that *is* quite a muscle..."

For weeks he'd been pushing himself down corridors, stubbornly refusing to even try an electric chair. "Thanks, but no thanks," he insisted. "This arm's the only good part left... can't let it deteriorate!" So upbeat and optimistic was he that there were times when friends or visitors were embarrassed to discover they had completely forgotten his physical condition. Instinctively holding out their right hand in greeting, they'd catch themselves with an awkward, "Oh, Bill, I'm sorry—I forgot you can't shake with your right hand." To which he would nod with a gracious grin and say something like, "Right back at you," and stick out his left one.

The Irishman Gets His Girl

The more Marilyn got to know Bill, the more she discovered that she was beginning to have some very non-professional feelings about her relationship with this upbeat Irishman. Each morning she looked forward to seeing him at his exercise sessions. On one occasion, in fact, when a change in hospital scheduling dropped his appointment, she found herself worried sick. She had to admit she was falling in love.

That was ridiculous! He was older, and a patient at that. Moreover, he was a Catholic, something that would surely rattle some family members. No, this was just an infatuation with his winning ways, she rationalized. Nothing more. Anyway, he probably didn't feel the same way about her. But was she reading too much into that intense way he had of looking at her?

Her answer came a few days later, after he had been uncharacteristically grumpy during the therapy session. "Please, Marty, forgive my sour comments today," he wrote in a note. It was signed, "Love, Curly Bill." When she saw the way he signed the card, her heart did a little flip. She *was* special to him!

The timing of all this was bad, she told herself. Right now there was something monumentally important that she must concern herself with—the state licensing exam she was scheduled to take soon. How on earth would she be able to concentrate on all she was required to study? "You can't imagine all the crazy Latin medical names I have to know," she had complained to Bill. "Muscles. Nerves. Functions. I'll never remember them all."

"Sure you will!" he countered, "I'll help you."

There then ensued a very unusual concerted "team effort." Every morning Marilyn would leave page upon page of medical data, along with piles of index cards. After therapy Bill spent most of the day typing study cards, using the "solitary index finger method." It was tedious all right, and boring— until he slipped in an original:

MUSCLE GROUP: DONNELIEF SCREAMATORIUM
                          PAINUS
With subgrouping of RELAXOR CRINGEMINITUS
ORIGIN: TOPAHEADUS FROM BOTTOM
                          OF FOOTEUS
                          (Caused by THERAPIST MEANUS)
NERVE: HOWLIN' HURLYITIS (named
                          after "Hurly," a stroke victim known
                          for screaming and howling when
                          having therapy.)

Their courtship lasted a year and a half. During that time Bill moved to a nursing home, where Marilyn would come on her days off to play records or push Bill's wheelchair near the Charles River for a romantic picnic. Sometimes she rented a car for day trips. Serious talk of marriage necessarily revolved around practical details of adapting to "regular" living on a daily basis... and, of course, religion.

Bill found seemingly simple solutions to the first problem. "We'll only make it if I pull my load," he stipulated adamantly. "I can dust and vacuum and even cook. And I promise, angel, you'll have a cup of tea and a light on when you come home from work."

Once Bill's role as househusband was mutually agreed on, they tackled the religion question and arrived at a compromise in which each promised never to proselytize the other. Both a priest and a minister would officiate at their ecumenical wedding. When they returned from their honeymoon, Bill decided to buy a "home altar" with a bronze crucifix and candles—as a personal reminder that Jesus was the source of all their strength and love. And so it was to remain through nearly twenty-five years of marriage.

After the Honeymoon...

As they had anticipated, there were complex adjustments—infinitely more than in most marriages—but the same need for compromise and "giving in" 100 percent at times.

"Why do you get your Irish up when I'm just ten minutes late?" Marilyn would ask before realizing that he was worried about her, not just being hard-headed about keeping their schedule. And it was Bill who volunteered not to be "so heavy on the beer." He sensed the danger of "boredom drinking," especially on hearing the constant question from relatives or friends, "What on earth do you do all day?"

"People think I sit here and count flowers on the wallpaper," he'd say, "Twenty-four just aren't enough hours for all I *want* to do in a day!"

In time his varied accomplishments certainly attested to this. He designed the family room in their house, and gained an enviable reputation in the neighborhood for the tomatoes that he grew on the porch. His intellectual pursuits, however, surprised not only others but himself as well. Because he was not a natural scholar, Bill would have quit high school had his dad not threatened with paternal finality, "You'll finish, Bill, even if you have to graduate with your six-year-old niece!"

Confined to the wheelchair, he developed an interest not only in current events and the news, but history as well. Bible study, theology texts, and anything relating to religion and western civilization captured his curiosity. A retired college professor used to drop by regularly just to "chew the rag about important things." In time Bill's home library became quite a useful resource, not only for his personal interest but for others as well.

"Bill, bet you don't know of a place where three major world religions used to worship in the same church," a friend challenged once on returning some books she had borrowed on biblical archeology.

"You mean Hebron, over in Israel? Sure... it started with the Jewish synagogue built over the gravesite of Abraham. When the crusaders came they enlarged it, making it a Catholic church. Then the Moslems just built a mosque over the whole thing!"

Bill's knowledge of general history once proved to be the catalyst for healing a bad relationship. It was with an elderly relative of Marilyn's, an avid reader of history, who had initially been so opposed to her marriage because of Bill's religion. He had avoided speaking to Bill at all. But the joking history buff won him over, especially after he began doing Marilyn's family genealogy!

All of this, however, did not diminish Bill's persistent concern about Marilyn. He did not want her to burn out because of him. He constantly encouraged her to take short trips on her own and was always teasing her about the women in her Town Garden Club. "Going off with your 'spadeyhoes,' eh? Gonna beautify the firehouse flower bed?" Later, Marilyn and Bill buckled down to medical books once more, and Marilyn earned her master's degree in pulmonary therapy. He was particularly proud the day she was honored by the hospital where she worked with an award for humanitarian service.

A highly enjoyable period in their lives came when both were involved in CB radio. He took the handle, "The Old Flounder" and she was "Sheltie Three," the name of one of their dogs. They would compete on trivia questions as she drove to and from work each day. He'd also advise her on weather and road conditions from the latest radio reports. He then tapped into banter with other CB enthusiasts with whom he came to form some rewarding friendships. Sometimes they took over his care and picked him up to play cards in one of their homes. On one occasion, when these fellows heard that one of Bill's dogs had died, they came to the door with a new pup—plus provisions for a full year!

Among many visiting friends, however, there was ill-disguised pity when they tried to identify with his lifestyle. "Don't you feel awfully cooped up, Bill?" they'd wonder aloud.

"Not really," he'd say, aware that his condition seemed to mandate such pity. "Relatives swing by, especially my brother Joe. They take me to the family's summer place. And the neighbors, they're great. They even get me to the Irish pub once a year!"

His way of "thinking healthy" went far beyond himself. It was evidenced, for example, when he felt it far better not to go somewhere. "Now let's be honest, my wheelchair would clutter up that small reception room. I'd be a nuisance!" or "I'm not scared of that flight of stairs! I just don't want you guys breaking your backs to lift me."

When it came to those handicapped who considered unreasonable demands their right simply because they were disabled, he could be quite impatient. "You can't punish other people just because they're healthy!"

Despite some minor ailments through the years, Bill insisted that he needed no daytime help. He was comfortable with the daily routine, beginning when Marilyn made coffee and their oldest dog, Angus, sat at his feet begging for pieces of toast. Only twice did he have to resort to Lifeline or call the police. "Guess I shouldn't have leaned so far," he conceded with a sheepish grin, pinned to the floor by his tipped wheelchair.

There were, however, two non-negotiable times of the day which were "chiseled in concrete." After breakfast dishes were done and necessary calls made—FISH (an ecumenical volunteer group which he directed by phone), business, or requests on the parish prayer line—he always joined in the Mass on TV.

At exactly noon he always kept the line free for a call from his "angel." It was Marilyn's way of checking in on him and sharing information. When they finished, however, they did not say "good-bye" to each other. Instead it was "three little words!"—their code for "I love you!"

Faith in the Face of Disability

Although Bill received the sacraments from the parish priest each month, he could not attend Sunday Mass. As he put it, "I save my energy for my friends' funerals! Their souls could use lots of prayer!"

Bill's deep love of people and instant empathy for those in crisis situations became evident when he was asked to serve as co-director of the prayer line. Calls were relatively frequent and encompassed many serious problems. Parishioners called to ask prayer for themselves, their families, and friends—everything from day-old infants clinging to life and accident victims in comas to patients going through heart surgery or an organ transplant. Whatever the call, Bill invariably responded "God bless 'er" or "God bless 'im" in such a compassionate tone the caller was sure there'd be intercession.

Bill was especially moved when his two-year-old nephew was diagnosed with cancer and underwent a bone marrow transplant. Hope ebbed, though, when the procedure failed. When the little boy died, Bill concluded with a big sigh, "Well, now the Donnellys have their own special little 'angel' in heaven." As in his own case, he did not challenge the mind of the Almighty One. People often told Bill they doubted God's justice and thought he had every right to demand an answer to the question "Why me?" He would merely ask, "Why *not* me?"

Year after year, Bill's spiritual vitality was honed and strengthened, even while he was fully aware of his human faults. "At times we could have brained each other!" Marilyn recalls with a laugh. "But from the beginning, we made a point of never going to bed mad."

Though healthy in soul, the time came when his medical condition began to deteriorate. For months he had been slipping and was not his usual, extroverted self.

Then came the day when he was called with a prayer line request, but his voice was so shaky and weak that it caused the caller to comment: "You sound like you should be on the prayer line yourself. Want me to pass it on?" For a moment he hesitated, unaccustomed to the role reversal. He had been so intent on praying for others that he had never considered the day might come when he would need the intercession of others. *My problems aren't that serious,* he thought to himself. *Why should the group rally around me?*

But he stopped himself. *Then again, why NOT me?*

"Okay, go ahead," he answered weakly.

The Homecoming

Marilyn insisted that he see a doctor. Early medical tests suggested the possibility of hepatitis. Two days later he was dead. After a life of heroic courage and inspiration, the Lord had given Bill what he had referred to as "the perfect healing." No more struggles, no limitations, and a final answer to all possible questions—especially the big "Why?"

His entire life, particularly his faith, left an indelible mark on Marilyn. She could not believe that such a vibrant personality would not somehow continue to have life in God's presence. These inner convictions coincided with Catholic teaching on the Communion of Saints and, within a year, Bill's faithful "angel" enrolled in R.C.I.A. and was received into the Church.

Marilyn expresses great inner peace now as she explains her gratitude that Bill went so quickly and that God took him first. "Otherwise it would have been very hard on him." She is convinced, furthermore, that he is now with the Lord, interceding for her. "In a way that is hard to explain, I just know he is praying for me. Even in the middle of some big problem, I am suddenly aware of what I should do and I am absolutely filled with peace."

Being alone was incredibly difficult, she admits, even two years after his death. "People sometimes comment, 'Well... now you don't have all that work with Bill.' They don't understand how much I miss him. Bill was God's gift to me. He was a living example of the power of hope."

Setting Things Straight

How many times have we been told that our situation is "just too much" to live with? Or how many times have even well-meaning people implied that—if they were in our shoes—they could not expend so much effort just to get through the day because it was not worth it?

We must not be swayed by pity! In effect, we should learn as soon as possible to put a mental "hold" on allowing ourselves to be weighed on some kind of fitness scale. After all, our problem is not necessarily permanent, nor is it *impossible* to enjoy a good deal of life—regardless of the obvious challenges.

Life has inestimable value—whatever its limitations—and deserves utmost respect from conception to the grave. We are instinctively aware that each human being is unique and is irreplaceable. That awareness, however, is being obliterated with lightning speed in our contemporary society.

Years before legalized abortion I was hospitalized in a Long Island hospital. My roommate was a woman who was having a second-trimester abortion. She thought she *might* have had measles in her third month of pregnancy—and so she and her dentist husband had persuaded the board of the hospital to allow this "procedure." As this woman and I talked through a good part of the night, I felt like someone who was trying to snatch the sweaty hand of a mother as she tried to hurl her child over a cliff because, "Just in case, how would it look to my husband's patients if there is a handicapped child in the yard?"

Legalized abortion has paved the way to our society's acceptance of death as the cleanest and most expedient answer to eliminating unwanted people. The Pied Pipers of assisted suicide are luring us to choose our "right" of self-destruction, especially if we are old or impaired. How soon, too many fail to consider, will that "right" become a "duty"?

One of the propaganda films used in the 1930s to soften the German people and make euthanasia a medical norm was a poignant film called *I Confess.* In this movie a young doctor comes home to give his beautiful wife a lethal injection as an act of supreme "love" because she has been diagnosed with multiple sclerosis. In the adjoining room, an empathetic colleague is softly playing Bach on the piano.

The scenario was portrayed with great class—nothing like death in Kevorkian's rusted-out van. It was a four-hanky tug of counterfeit compassion. But the intent and message are precisely the same as Dr. Death's: Some life is not worth living.

As one who has lived with MS for forty-seven years, I understand fully the limitations of a chronic illness. And yet, I have also been blessed with an intense awareness of how precious life really is. Both my husband and I were diagnosed as "infertile." My first son, "a medical impossibility," is now a molecular biologist.

When I became pregnant with our second son, the doctor tried to persuade me to abort him because the pregnancy could exacerbate my multiple sclerosis. When I refused, I was told to find another doctor. Happily, my disease instead went into remission for seven years following that pregnancy. During that time, three of my full-length dramas were produced off-Broadway. *Reunion of Sorts* contained a strong pro-life theme and was based partly on my hospital encounter with the dentist's wife. Today I have much to be thankful for (including five grandchildren!); I have experienced time and again the healing hand of God and the healing power of hope.

There are times, of course, when God chooses not to heal us of our physical limitations. Like Old Flounder, there are those who must adapt their lifestyles to cope with a disability. Not all of the severely restricted can overcome their conditions on a physical level. If you are facing this situation, take heart. You can still live a full and vital life if you guard your mental and spiritual well-being, like Bill did. Guilt trips and complaining will only add to your burden. However, if you "look to the light," you can embrace life with a sense of real joy!

Looking to the Light

In the final analysis, both the suffering and the perfectly healthy among us must accept the fact that there are countless mishaps in life. We may think we are immune because we are young, eat right, put a lot of time into aerobics and other exercise, or get plenty of sleep. In the end, though, all of us will need the help of God somewhere along the line.

The chronically and terminally ill can find a renewed sense of hope if they learn to rely on God for the strength they need each day. This reliance is perhaps best illustrated by the following dream/allegory:

Footprints*

One night a man had a dream. He dreamed he was walking along the beach with the Lord. Across the sky flashed scenes from his life. Sometimes he noticed two sets of footprints in the sand.

One set of prints were his own.

The other set, he knew, were the Lord's.

Other times the man noticed only one set of footprints. He was amazed to discover that these were usually the very lowest and saddest times in his life. This really bothered the man, and he questioned the Lord about it.

"Lord, you said that once I decided to follow you, you'd walk with me all the way. But I have noticed that during the most troublesome times in my life, there is only one set of footprints. I don't understand—when I needed you the most, why did you leave me?"

The Lord replied, "*My precious, precious child, I love you and I would never leave you. During your times of trial and suffering, when you see only one set of footprints, it was then that I carried you.*"

*Author unknown

Follow-Up Action

Our faith clearly tells us that it is not enough to simply assert "I believe." Our actions must show it. Psychologists likewise look to appropriate action once a patient has grasped his or her problem. We can first begin in our decision to "affirm life" with the following:

1. Learn all you can about your disorder and put all this information on the "shelf" of your mind.

Question your doctors. Read books about your condition. Compile as much reasonable and objective information as possible. This will help to calm the fears and uncertainties that come from not knowing the truth. However, don't become obsessed about your illness. Use the bits of information as you would use reference books, taking them down only when needed. Decide not to dwell on your problem constantly, confusing fact with subjective emotions.

2. Develop your own personal prayer life.
A positive faith-attitude is a form of therapy that can be every bit as important and powerful as the treatment your doctor prescribes. It is the seed of all hope. The simplest prayer bolsters faith. If you need a "prayer starter," try this "Modern Novena of Hope."

A Modern Novena of Hope

Day One
Each day for nine days begin your prayer with the text noted below, and follow with an Our Father, a Hail Mary, and a Glory Be. Finish each day's prayer with the concluding prayer on page 34. May the familiar words of these prayers give you great comfort in stressful times!

Heavenly Father, you have created a universe so vast it cannot be measured. You have carefully planned and prepared for all life, including my own. You have sent your Son to ransom me from my sins. No matter what my problems, therefore, I will believe that all things are possible with you. For you are God!

Prayer to be repeated each day: For God alone my soul waits in silence, for my hope is from him (Ps 62:5).

Our Father, who art in heaven, hallowed be thy name. Thy kingdom come; thy will be done, on earth as it is in heaven. Give us this day our daily bread. Forgive us our trespasses as we forgive those who trespass against us. And lead us not into temptation but deliver us from evil. Amen.

Hail Mary, full of grace, the Lord is with thee. Blessed art thou among women and blessed is the fruit of thy womb, Jesus. Holy Mary, Mother of God, pray for us sinners, now, and at the hour of our death. Amen.

Glory be to the Father, and to the Son, and to the Holy Spirit. As it was in the beginning, is now, and ever shall be, world without end. Amen.

Concluding Prayer:

Let me not forget, my ever-loving Lord, that you will never abandon me. I am never totally alone. You are always waiting for me to direct my attention to you. I may not understand your ways many times, but I will not doubt that your intentions for me are the best. United with you, we are a majority!

Day Two

Loving Lord, what a privilege it is to belong to you! I have been "connected" simply by being baptised as a Christian. Let me realize that this has put an indelible "mark" on my very self. It makes me your child. I have an eternal inheritance—one I do not want to miss. In my pain now, just hold my hand. "For God alone..." Our Father... Hail Mary... Glory Be... Let me not forget...

Day Three

Lord Jesus, you willingly became human like me, and you willingly died on a cross. You know what suffering is like. Your heart was always filled with compassion and love, and you have not changed. You sent your Holy Spirit to live in me all the days of my life, no matter how bad things seem today. "For God alone..." Our Father... Hail Mary... Glory Be... Let me not forget...

Day Four

Holy Spirit, Jesus said you would come and be my helper. He knew I would make wrong choices in life. He knew how the Devil would make me feel discouraged and even despair over sickness, and betrayal, over weakness and broken promises. Please help me right now, lift me from this abyss of hopelessness. "For God alone..." Our Father... Hail Mary... Glory Be... Let me not forget...

Day Five

Holy Spirit, you are the counselor whom Jesus promised before he ascended to Heaven. You have the wisdom I need to know God's will in my situation. I get so confused. Help me to hear you "speak" when I read Scripture. Teach me how to "be still" as you open my mind and my heart to what you want me to do. "For God alone..." Our Father... Hail Mary... Glory Be... Let me not forget...

Day Six

There are times, precious Holy Spirit, when the thing I need most is to have you console me. There is an emptiness and pain in my heart that only God can remedy. Let me understand that worldly answers all fall short in the end. So shower the graces Jesus earned that I may have courage and perseverance. "For God alone..." Our Father... Hail Mary... Glory Be... Let me not forget...

Day Seven

Spirit of God, Jesus said you would guide me. More and more, I see how much I need to be guided. I beg of you, make it clear how I can grow in sincere love for God and for all people. Teach me to be pure in body and mind. Give me supernatural strength to accept whatever you allow in my life. "For God alone..." Our Father... Hail Mary... Glory Be... Let me not forget...

Day Eight

You are called the Paraclete, Holy Spirit, because you are the defender Jesus promised to each of us. You are like a celestial lawyer, arguing our case, convincing our hearts that God is really on our side. If I make a habit of calling on you to "speak up," I will not be overcome by negatives. "For God alone..." Our Father... Hail Mary... Glory Be... Let me not forget...

Day Nine

Triune God, I believe in you, Father, Son, and Holy Spirit. You are trustworthy. You are always "on the job." You never get weary or disgusted as I so often do. I want to follow a new path, the path of love. Jesus, this was your commandment. I accept with a grateful heart the faith and hope this brings. "For God alone..." Our Father... Hail Mary... Glory Be... Let me not forget...

3. Watch your attitude toward healthy people.

Nip any jealous or resentful thoughts in the bud. Do not punish healthy friends or family members simply because they can do things you cannot do.

4. Make a mental "life balance sheet."

Ask God to help you assess all the "working parts" you still have (physical, mental, and spiritual) and how to maximize the potential of each one.

5. Expect to be misunderstood and inadequately helped—even ignored at times.

Obviously, we do not live in a perfect world. The human condition leaves much to be desired in just about every area. So while we strive to live with or overcome some problem, it is self-defeating to stridently insist on our personal rights and needs at all cost. After all, life cannot stand still for others because we happen to be suffering. Remember Old Flounder—how can you put someone else's needs ahead of your own today?

The life of every human being is to be respected in an absolute way because man is the only creature on earth that God has "wished for himself."

Church in the Modern World, No. 24

TWO

Only One Life—
Here and Hereafter

For thou didst form my inward parts,
>   thou didst knit me together in my
>   mother's womb.
I praise thee, for thou art fearful and
>   wonderful...
Thy eyes beheld my unformed substance;
>   in thy book were written, every one of them,
the days that were formed for me,
>   when as yet there was none of them.

PSALMS 139:13-17

When someone was seriously ill in the Middle Ages, a priest was immediately summoned and church bells were rung. The simple folk of the time stopped their activities momentarily to pray for the individual. If the bells tolled later on, it informed the people of a death—two rings for a woman and three for a man.

"No man is an island entire of itself.... Any man's death diminishes me because I am involved in Mankind," John

Donne wrote. "Therefore never send to know for whom the bell tolls; it tolls for thee."

A new and ominous bell is tolling in modern times. Its enticing sound, however, is like an invisible vacuum sucking unsuspecting people into an imploding whirlpool. Unlike those medieval church bells, it is not used to spread the news of someone's death: it is Death itself!

Fancy imagery? Not really. Today's insidious bell is the twentieth century's most troubling phenomenon and its incredibly evil legacy: total disregard for the sanctity of human life.

That bell is enticing people to forget that our essential human nature is created and limited. We did not conceive ourselves, but we are each a unique creation of God. Our earthly lives will surely end, yet this all-loving Creator has destined us to live on with him for eternity.

Unlike anything in the animal or plant world that God created, we share his image uniquely in our freedom of will. The trouble is that we so often use it to make the wrong choices about the immense value of a single human life. Especially our own!

Setting Things Straight

A recent Annals of Internal Medicine study announced the introduction of SUPPORT, a medical computer to aid doctors in making prognoses regarding the outcome and risks of treatment. It was developed at George Washington University using information from four thousand terminally ill patients, and it is supposedly more accurate than the physicians themselves in determining quality of life.[1]

The term "quality of life" is like sweet-tasting poison. Not only is it horrendously misleading, but it puts up a smoke-screen between us and the God who made us, redeemed us, regenerated us, sustains us. Outside of God, who has the standard by which the quality of our lives can be measured? Who can be trusted to set this standard? Certainly not a computer programmed by imperfect professionals.

Turning the Tide for Life

In 1995, Dr. Joseph Stanton, who wrote the foreword for this book and is considered the godfather of the pro-life movement in the United States, sought to recapture the moral vision first encapsulated in the Hippocratic Oath. The oath has been omitted from medical school graduations across the country ever since it was dismissed in 1973 by Supreme Court Justice Harry Blackmun as "a Pythagorean manifesto and not the expression of an absolute standard of conduct."[2]

The original oath, in which doctors swore to "give no deadly medicine to anyone if asked, nor suggest any such counsel" and to refuse to give a woman an instrument to produce an abortion was not in keeping with the values American culture holds most dear: "a woman's right to choose" and the protection of our "quality of life."

The revised 1995 oath, which updated the language of the original, has received the strong support of many doctors and ethicists across the country, including Rabbi J. David Bleich, evangelical Protestant scholar Harold O.J. Brown, and William May, member of the papal theological commission. It has also drawn the support of such public figures as Dr. Edmund Pelligrino, director of the Kennedy Institute for Ethics at

Georgetown University and Dr. C. Everett Koop, former U.S. Surgeon General.[3] (The complete text of The 1995 Restated Hippocratic Oath is found in Appendix B of this book.)

The Quality of Life Defined

When considering the quality of life, there is much to consider apart from physical wholeness. We must also consider the mental, psychological, and spiritual aspects of life as well. Some people place too much emphasis on one area, striving for perfection in that aspect at the expense of other areas. For example, some may pursue intellectual pursuits at the expense of spiritual wholeness and develop a hard cynicism. Others, including at times the physically challenged, become so absorbed by achieving physical wholeness that they neglect other priorities. When this happens, an imbalance occurs.

We do not always bring this upon ourselves. Sometimes in the course of life things happen to us that bring about an imbalance in the various areas of our lives. We all have good days and bad days. There can be weeks, months, and even years when our mental, physical, or emotional state is poor. We may sometimes echo the prophet Elijah, who prayed, "It is enough now O Lord; take away my life!" (1 Kgs 19:1ff). It is a plea quickly forgotten, though, when we recover!

In essence, it is not so much what happens to us which ultimately determines our life quality, but our attitude towards it. There are those who refuse to doubt that there's always some kind of hope. Then there are the others who somehow feel that problem-free living is akin to a constitutional "right." Suffering, therefore, throws them into despair or rage at any perceived cause outside themselves. They cannot consider the power of God-given hope because God seems either irrelevant or impotent.

A Mature Understanding of Hope

As we mature psychologically and spiritually through the years, we come to see that God is present with the attributes of both a gentle father and a nurturing mother. He trains us in faith because it plays a key role in our attitude formation. Just as the demonstrated love of a human parent elicits a child's faith, God leads us to trust in him. Then our attitudes change and are refined. Like the charting on a graph, results gradually indicate more and more good days and fewer and fewer ones taken over by our shadow selves.

In the final analysis, the condition of anyone's life at the present moment should not be used as the criterion for judging its so-called "quality." Remember, the existing difficulty may not necessarily be a permanent condition. And even if the condition is a lasting one, this does not detract from the inherent value of life or what God can teach us through our weakness.

For the sake of illustration, let us examine the medical case histories of two women, each of whom has been afflicted with multiple sclerosis for several decades. Although each is married and has two living children, the women both have the chronic-progressive type of this crippling disease which now keeps them largely housebound. Along with their handicap, however, there are also numerous unrelated health problems which have plagued them as well.

The Case of Mary Doe

Growing up, Mary had a poor relationship with a non-affirming mother; she does not recall a single embrace. It led to a pattern of depression and negativity, which was only heightened with the onset of MS after only one year of marriage.

Six years, one child, and several miscarriages later, Mary became legally blind. Her attempt to learn Braille was futile since there was almost no sensation in her fingertips. Her gait was so poor that bi-annual hospital therapy ensued, including the experimental administration of intravenous histamine. Years later a doctor told her this had actually caused malignant tumors, which required surgery.

This was enough reason for self-pity and anger—not to mention the total paralysis that ensued with each severe respiratory infection. For up to two weeks she could swallow only liquids from a blender, usually prepared by her husband and a second son then in high school.

Mary has fallen repeatedly, breaking bones several times. She has had three concussions, the last resulting in sporadic optical brain seizures, when things seem as though seen through shattered glass for about a half an hour. She is now in a motorized wheelchair most of the day since, along with the MS, a badly arthritic knee causes the falls. She is gradually losing the use of her hands as well, and needs help to dress.

The Case of Jane Smith

Bouts of intense dizziness and leg tremors first signaled illness—years before her MS was diagnosed. Also, when her first baby was only five months old, she had a total loss of equilibrium and coordination. Though frightening, such episodes passed and the family picked up normal living, even taking vacations.

In time, Jane experienced extreme fatigue, along with distinct double vision which necessitated wearing an eyepatch. But this did not kill her creativity. (She was amused when a blinking eye she drew on her flesh-colored patch took people aback!) After chores were done and the family gone she undertook all kinds of artistic projects: customized birthday cakes and other creative projects, including several murals—a train on three walls of one son's bedroom and flower "murals" on the garage. All while using a six-inch magnifier!

Jane could touch-type, but could not read. Happily, a group of budding TV dramatists would bring her to their weekly adult education classes where her legs were lifted onto a hassock and someone else read her work. Once, having a great need to rest, she ended up in Sculpture I. By springtime, the eight pounds of wet clay she had come home with was formed into a bust of her husband. Her sole complaint? "His ears fell off in the kiln."

Jane wrote books, taught children religious education in her home, and with her husband, has led a parish prayer line for over twenty years. Her personal "prayer therapy" remains unchanged (interceding before God symptom by symptom).

After reading these two case histories, one is struck by Mary Doe's resigned helplessness in the face of a depressive mountain of obstacles over which she has no control. (Even half her problems would make many people today support a decision for assisted suicide!) Indeed, her "quality" of life seems as dismal as though chiseled in black concrete!

Conversely, Jane Smith is determined to extract joy by living life to the fullest, moment by moment, taking chances, finding creative outlets, and hoping for the best. She trusts in the future, where an all-powerful God can bring good even out of conditions that, *for the time being,* are quite bad.

However, there is a paradox in these histories. They are not the summarized records of two women with MS, but one. This I know with absolute certainty. How? They both belong to *me.*

Looking To The Light

Some years ago this bumper sticker caught my attention and made a lasting impression:
BE PATIENT. GOD'S NOT DONE WITH ME YET!

A thimbleful of theological wisdom!

We may not be able to see what God is trying to do for us in the midst of pain, weariness, confusion, discouragement, and reversals of all kinds. But he does have a plan for our lives, one leading to a goal that is totally incomprehensible to us now. He is preparing us to share his eternal bliss, with all those who have loved him through countless ages. This is the reason to keep on hoping, no matter what happens. It is like hoping for the sun on a miserable, stormy day. We know full well it is there, and we also know that, in time, it will come out again!

His plan or will for us, however, takes into account our free will, which he never usurps. There are many times in our lives when, in his omniscience, God has clear awareness of some disaster for which we are heading. Yet he allows it to happen because we are not robots. Then, like a loving parent, Our Lord makes every attempt to restructure our circumstances so that we become willing to make the correct choice at a later time. He can make all things—even our mistakes—work for good.

"God writes straight with crooked lines" is more than a philosophical truism. In a sense, God is a universal mapmaker who is perpetually drawing up fresh "life maps" for us. When we veer off the main throughway, he steers us on to bypasses and detours, always leading us back to the original destination.

Along with having the proper direction, we need clear vision. Jesus, "the light of the world" (Jn:8:12), must be our directional focus for, as he said, no follower of his needs to feel fear or stumble along alone. We can liken ourselves to a small child who cannot fall asleep without a night light, but who is not afraid to walk down a dark street—so long as she is clutching her father's hand. God walks with us through the darkest of times.

Once we are inwardly convinced beyond the shadow of a doubt that life is unique and that it is precious—be it an unborn child with some genetic abnormality or an octogenarian with dementia—then we can begin to see why God has gone to so much trouble for our salvation. We come to glean understanding of why he not only dignified us with his own image, but also sent his divine Son—the prototype of hope—after whom we can model our lives with utmost confidence.

St. Paul tells us that our faith lies precisely in being convinced about the reality of things which we do not see, and being inwardly confident about that for which we hope (see Hebrews 11:1). This is especially needed by those of us who are immersed in the grips of some inescapable suffering. Over and over, day after day, we must take a deep breath and choose to remind ourselves that God is still in charge and that—no matter what our feelings shout—we will somehow get through the difficulty. If need be, we must take it on nothing but "dry faith" that our loving Lord can and will work good out of everything.

Developing such hope and trust in God is not an instant personal accomplishment. It is, quite literally, a partnership that grows and develops throughout a lifetime as we gradually learn to "let go and let God."

It has been my privilege to have witnessed the powerful and sometimes unexpected effects as I have handed the reins of my life over to God. Those two "case histories" of mine—lived out in dovetail fashion—were intended as a candid example of this. Like a yo-yo, I repeatedly slackened in hope and trust as I would try taking over. Just as repeatedly, Jesus would draw me back, making my faith like a taut string once more.

God has his ways! Primary among them is a powerful survival instinct that can make heroic humans out of the worst of emotional jellyfish. We instinctively shield ourselves from danger or run for cover because he intended that we value and protect our gift of life. It follows naturally then that we do whatever possible to see that the same protection be given to others—beginning with the most defenseless among us, the unborn.

Beyond basic survival, we have innumerable human needs through which God also reaches us and uses for our training in faith. The problem is that we are continuously confusing needs with wants. When we plead, therefore, for what we think we need we must resign ourselves to the fact that he will answer in *his* way, and according to *his* timetable, not ours. So it makes simple sense to let go, to relinquish our preferences and willingly defer to this infinite wisdom and power.

What a joy it can be when we finally wait in confident trust, expecting our wonderful Lord to act! Time and again he strengthens us beyond what strength we think we have. He alters circumstances, and softens hitherto brittle hearts. He gives us the wisdom to lift others who are low and in whom we can see our old selves. He fills us with peace and joy, a peace really beyond understanding. Finally, he gives us a genuine victory over the fear of death.

There is a classic prayer by Cardinal John Newman that has been invaluable to me and countless others, puts all this into perspective. I was first introduced to it by a young priest who chose it for his ordination prayer.

Many years ago, when the disturbing symptoms of MS were making me feel utterly unproductive, I began to sob during confession. The priest, who had graduated from seminary only six months before, asked that I wait for him in the sacristy after giving me absolution. Since there was only one more penitent, it did not take him long to get to me.

"Meditate on this prayer," he advised. "It's one of the things that has helped me. I don't know how I would have made it through the seminary without Cardinal Newman."

Prayer of Cardinal Newman

God has created me to do him some definite service;
He has committed some work to me
   which he has not committed to another.
I have my mission—
I may never know it in this life,
   but I shall be told it in the next.
I am a link in a chain, a bond of connection
   between persons.
He has not created me for naught,
I shall do good. I shall do his work.
I shall be an angel of peace,
   a preacher of truth in my own place
   while not intending it.
If I but keep his commandments.
Therefore, I will trust him.
Whatever, wherever I am, I can never be thrown away.
If I am in sickness, my sickness may serve him;
If I am in sorrow, my sorrow may serve him.
He does nothing in vain. He knows what he is about.
He may take away my friends.
He may throw me among strangers
He may make me feel desolate,
Make my spirits sink,
Hide my future from me—
Still he knows what he is about.

Follow-Up Action

Dr. Leo Alexander, world-renowned neuro-psychiatrist and U.S. consultant at the Nuremberg war crimes trials, wrote, "The Lord Jesus Christ not only stands as creator of remarkable cures but also stands revealed as possibly the earliest psycho-physiologist, in that he recognized the role which the patient plays in the accomplishment of such cures."[4]

So where do we start doing our part? How can our attitudes be healed?

1. Ask the Holy Spirit to help you assess your thought patterns.

Are your thoughts primarily on yourself... and are they almost always negative and hopeless? Have you conditioned yourself to expect the worst of people and problems? Are you habitually critical? (No rationalizing here!)

2. In your mind, picture Jesus as the Good Shepherd.

He is coming toward you holding an injured lamb on his shoulders. In a simple, conversational way, tell him that you too need to be held like that, that you want to learn how to trust in him. Ask him to help you relax, not to blame others for your difficulty, but to instill instead his peace and joy in you. Then thank him and believe it done.

3. Start being as positive and hopeful as possible.

As soon as a negative thought steals into your mind, stop it with a good memory. Concentrate on that memory in detail. Relish it. No matter how insignificant you may consider the memory, tell God how much you appreciate it.

4. Speak up for life!

It may seem intimidating at first, but you should tell your family, friends, doctors, or health care providers how much you value God's gift of life to you. Let them be clearly aware that you do not believe in assisted suicide, no matter what your age or physical condition. Tell them you are hoping to be healed, but that you want to live only as long as God wants—and that he alone has the right to determine when that will be.

Suffering is present in the world in order to release love, in order to give birth to works of love toward neighbor, in order to transform the whole of human civilization into a "civilization of love."

Pope John Paul II
"On the Christian Meaning of Human Suffering,"
Par. 54

THREE

Why Must I Suffer?

More than that, we rejoice in our sufferings, knowing that suffering produces endurance, and endurance produces character, and character produces hope, and hope does not disappoint us, because God's love has been poured into our hearts through the Holy Spirit which has been given to us.

ROMANS 5:3-5

Unlike her siblings, Shirley had a problem with drugs from her early years. Despite a high I.Q., she managed to finish high school only on spurts of self-determination. By the time she was out of college, drinking seemed to fit in with her liberated lifestyle as well.

"You're killing yourself... I can't believe you got so immoral," her father said sadly on one of her rare visits home. "It's good your mother isn't alive to see this. We raised you right, took you to church with all of us... why don't you marry this fellow you're living with?"

"Come out of the Middle Ages, Dad!" she would laugh, "but if it makes you feel better, just keep praying. Say a novena or something for me!"

Within six months she was pregnant, her boyfriend gone.

The years that followed were a nightmare for her—she had to face detox centers and lost jobws. The relationships in her life suffered, as well. She was in and out of temporary relationships with men, being on bad terms with her brothers and sisters (her father now gone).

But the worst was her son's obvious disdain. At sixteen he told her, "Soon's I get some money, I'm out of here! You don't know the meaning of the word 'mother'!"

It was the afternoon she sat in a doctor's office, waiting for the results of lab tests, that a sudden awareness engulfed her whole being. Everything was going to change for the worse—and it would be out of her hands.

"I'm sorry, Shirley," the doctor began, "You have a rather advanced lung cancer." She was speechless as he detailed the course of action that seemed most appropriate.

It took almost a year to recuperate from surgery. She lost her hair and became quite heavy after chemotherapy. Then the doctor discovered a new malignancy in her brain and she had to have radiation. Months later, assured that she was completely cured, she knocked on the door of a church rectory, asking if the priest had "plenty of time."

For years she had wanted to come back to the church... only God could make sense of her life anymore, she knew that. But it wasn't until the night she got down on her knees and sobbed, "I can't go on any more. Help me, Jesus," that everything changed. She had a great desire to go to confession, to finally turn her life around. This she began to do the very next day.

"Guess it took God to hit me over the head!" Shirley later concluded. "Should have done it much sooner... but I kept blaming him for the mess I'd put myself in."

Those immersed in the values of our secular culture have no understanding of discomfort or suffering from a spiritual perspective. Unfortunately, neither do a great many who profess to be Christian but who are just as misled, confused, and self-seeking.

We easily succumb to the notion that some cruel, impersonal fate is the cause of our difficulty. Whether coping with an ulcer or partial post-stroke paralysis, many of us feel like limp puppets being ruthlessly jerked around by a divine puppeteer.

Throughout human history people have always been haunted and perplexed by the existence of suffering. (Note the biblical laments of Job, whose patient understanding was a long time in coming!) Small wonder then that so many people swallow the belief that God is far off—busy running the universe—and unaware of their pain. Worse yet, they may conclude that he knows, but is really powerless in dire circumstances.

Nothing could be further from the truth! Whether we believe it or not, we could not continue our existence for one more breath were it not for God's passionate love for us. His caring commitment was clearly evidenced with the Jews, his chosen people. Time after time he snatched them from the jaws of idolatry, guiding them, sending them prophets to lead them on the path of righteousness. He gave them unique dignity and established them as a nation from whom he intended to take the human component of the Messiah.

The God of the New Testament, moreover, is the same loving Savior who comes to heal both body and mind and who, after his own suffering and death on a cross, is forever alive—pointing a way through our pain and wretchedness. He utilizes suffering and gives it spiritual worth. Francois Mauriac, the Nobel prize-winning author whom *Time* magazine called "an artist of astonishing power," attested to this. In a recorded eulogy to be released after his death, he said, "I believe as I did as a child, that life has meaning, direction, and value; that no suffering is lost; that every tear and each drop of blood counts; and that the secret of the world is to be found in St. John's 'Deus caritas est'—'God is love.'"[1]

Setting Things Straight

As previously noted, if we had it our way, there would be no such thing as personal suffering—unless we are masochistic or mentally unbalanced. Basically, we are all cowards, especially when faced with intense and unremitting pain. A simple tobogganing accident in college—resulting in ripped knee tendons—first confirmed this for me! My friends and I were on a remote hill in Michigan, several hours from the nearest doctor. There was *nothing* to ease the pain.

Certainly we call out to God in our misery, whether loudly or inaudibly. We want him to be an instant super medical technocrat or the bearer of a new and improved antibiotic or miracle drug. It might be the monotonous throbbing that wrings our body from within, or the dry heaves of nausea, or the stabbing red-hot-poker pain that seems totally intolerable... but then suddenly increases.

C.S. Lewis said, "God whispers to us in our pleasures but shouts to us in our pains, it is his megaphone to rouse a dead world."[2]

In this regard we are hardly alone. St. Paul, after some extraordinary revelations, wrote, "And to keep me from being too elated by the abundance of revelations, a thorn was given me in the flesh, a messenger of Satan, to harass me, to keep me from being too elated. Three times I besought the Lord about this, that it should leave me; but he said to me, 'My grace is sufficient for you, for my power is made perfect in weakness.' I will all the more gladly boast of my weaknesses, that the power of Christ may rest upon me... for when I am weak, then I am strong" (2 Cor 12:7-10).

Is this just spiritual double talk? Hardly. The basic thing Scripture conveys is that God is the supreme power, and that both healing and suffering are a mystery in his plan of redemption. In our puny, finite minds, we always strive for independence, and believe ourselves capable of engineering our own well-being. It is usually only when we are weak and totally helpless that we acknowledge and implore God's supernatural intervention.

"Circumstances that rip out the walls of our self-sufficiency are God's blessings in disguise," writes Merlin Carothers, author of the classic, *Power in Praise*. "We can truly thank God... and praise him for every blow that removes more of the illusion that we have the ability to handle our own situation."[3]

To begin with, we must stop blaming God for all our troubles. Without the entrance of sin into the world, suffering as we know it simply would not exist. It was not God's idea, but the work of Satan. It is humanity's rebellion against God which brought the inevitable effects of disease, illness, pain, and death.

"...God did not make death, and he does not delight in the death of the living. For he created all things that they might exist... " (Wis 13:14).

The evil of suffering comes through the original sin of mankind as well through our personal sin and the sins of others. Even social sins—discrimination, exploitation of the poor, escalating violence—all begin with individual wrongdoing. What is more, such evils as greed, slander, and sexual abuse are often carried across generations.

Though the tide of sin is strong, we must never forget the immensity of God's power coming against evil. Yes, suffering is a reality of life and everyone endures some measure of it, but as Christians we know that wherever there is great evil there is also the potential for even greater good.

Take the drive-by shooting of a five-year-old boy in one large city, for instance, which brought out a show of community sharing and cooperation that ultimately evicted drug dealers from that neighborhood. The parents of that little boy have, without a doubt, suffered intense pain. But whether they are aware of it or not, Jesus was suffering along with them. It is in pain that we become most like him, for when we take up our personal crosses and follow him, we come to understand that we too must be "perfected" in suffering as he was (see Hebrews 2:10). If we allow Jesus to use our suffering in his perfect plan, we become joined with him in what Dr. Albert Schweitzer described as a universal "brotherhood of pain."

It would be very easy, in all honesty, to reserve this brotherhood for only stoics, religious neurotics, or full-blown saints. After all, there are many good people who call themselves "Christian" but who are embarrassed by Jesus' cross and all that it implies for us. They contend that a God of love would not want to immerse himself in human suffering, but would want to eliminate it. Yes... and no.

In his initial plan for those whom God created—in his perfect will—there would be no war between the best and the worst of human impulses, therefore no disobedience, mistrust, or sin. So there would be no need for suffering, and no need for a Savior. The human condition, however, calls immeasurably more often for his permissive will instead. Because of our free will he allows many things which do not conform to his perfect will.

That permissive will of God's can be to our liking or not. When things are going along smoothly, or when we recover from our illnesses or accidents in record time, who do we tend to credit? The flu shot we took? Greater resistance because of a highly nutritional diet or jogging? Or the God who permitted all these attempts at health to work?

Only in heaven will we learn of the countless times that our bodies and minds were healed through his loving permission, many times even without our being aware that something was wrong! It's like the automatic rerouting of our telephone call when the master computer detects problems—even while we are speaking on the phone and have no suspicion of trouble.

Conversely, our loving Lord can employ his permissive will to draw out much good, even though we may be broken. When a believer remains adamantly faithful in the midst of pain and all kinds of reversals, it can be a powerful demonstration of supernatural power. This gives great glory to God.

Questions still remain. Why do pious God-fearing people suffer while others who are not leading upright lives do not? Why do children get cancer? Why are the innocent plagued and oppressed with so much suffering and deprivation while blatant sinners get off scot-free?

We simply do not know. We cannot possibly understand the ultimate reason God allows all this. Yet, if we believe his Word, what he allows to happen is not haphazard or random—as the existentialist playwrights accused in their *Theatre of the Absurd.* Contending that life is pointless and without plan, they had theatrical "experiences"—extemporaneous dialogue or plays with no plots.

We must continually remind ourselves, therefore, that God knows us by name, that he holds us "in the palm of his hand," and that he has a plan for our lives. He wastes nothing. Like an efficient manager, he makes use of everything for our eternal well-being.

Looking to the Light

Our loving Savior knows all about our pains and woes down to the smallest detail. The Man of Sorrows is fully acquainted with distress, with sleeplessness, with constant misunderstanding, with disappointment, and with ultimate betrayal by a close friend. In his glorified state, therefore, interceding as he is for us before the Father in heaven, his heart is still moved with empathy and compassion.

His loving concern has not diminished one iota since he walked the earth and freely extended his healing touch to all those who were brought to him—dead or alive. In time, however, all who were restored to wholeness grew old, got sick again, and died—even if they did become believers. In the end, Jesus gave to them—just as he does to us—an invitation to share in his crucifixion, where he conquered sin and death.

This theological truth became a stark reality to me many years ago after major surgery. Medication seemed ineffective for the first hour after regaining consciousness in the hospital recovery section. I writhed in agony without so much as moving a muscle. My eyes slowly focused on the crucifix on the other side of my room and I silently cried out, "This pain doesn't make any sense!" I felt instantly a part of Jesus' suffering on the cross, and he reassured me, "My crucifixion made no sense either... before Easter."

Our shared suffering gave me a kind of Easter assurance and inner peace, even though the pain remained. When I accepted Jesus' invitation to suffer with him vicariously on the cross, then he could heal my unexpressed terror and rage over being totally helpless.

Whether we give our permission or not, Jesus can use our suffering to put us in the right place before him. Often it is the only effective tool for bringing down our false defenses, for humbling us and making us realize that, no matter how great our efforts, we are not the final masters of our destiny.

Sometimes it is just impossible for us to grasp how vain and selfish we are until our plans are crumbled, our dreams shattered, and we are hurting in body, mind, and spirit. When time goes by, however, and we reflect on the experience, we discover how really dependent we are. In addition, though we would certainly prefer not to relive it again, the bad experience has prepared us to face with confidence the next pain or trouble or anguish which will most assuredly come along.

For centuries spiritual masters referred to this whole process as "purification," "purgation," or "the way to perfection." St. John of the Cross indicates that in suffering: "...the soul is as powerless in this case as one who has been imprisoned in a dark dungeon... until the spirit is humbled, softened and purified, and grows so keen and delicate and pure that it can become one with the Spirit of God."[4]

Only for the very spiritual? Not if we believe Terry Anderson, who was an American hostage in Lebanon for seven years. He said, "I think that we come closest to God at our lowest moments. It's easier to hear him when you are stripped of pride, arrogance, when you have nothing to rely on except him. It's pretty painful to get to that point, and that's when you come closest to despair. But when you do, he's there, and that's what keeps you from going any further."[5] Suffering can transform us, perfect us, and unite us simply because we participate in fellowship with Christ.

A Prayer of Surrender

Lord, I feel at the end of my rope. Nothing seems to work for me anymore. I'm sick of being sick and discouraged. Jesus, I have finally come to realize that you really are "the Way and the Truth and the Life" and that you suffered and died for me personally. I thank you sincerely, despite my unworthiness. Please forgive all the sins of my life. I am truly sorry for them. I surrender my life to you this day. I ask you to be the Lord of my life from now on... no matter what. I give you my past, which is washed clean in your blood. I give you my future life, for however long you plan. I give you this present moment in faith and trust. Nothing can ever separate me from your love. Nothing. With all my heart I praise you, Jesus, and I thank you. My Lord and my God, you are my hope and salvation.

Follow-up Action

1. Reprogram your spiritual computer.

Instead of succumbing to the old "poor me" habit, replace your grumbling with, "Praise you, Jesus; thank you, Jesus; may this be to your glory." Feelings are irrelevant. Just repeat this little prayer of trust and the positive thoughts will drive out the negative, destructive ones. According to St. Francis DeSales, when little bees are caught in a storm, they take hold of small stones in order to keep their balance when they fly. A simple prayer of praise (an acknowledgment of God's sovereignty) can be our source of stability. Through it we say "yes" to God, believing we will not be blown away in the terrible winds of life.

2. Eliminate principal sources of negativity.

Stop watching too much TV, especially amoral talk shows. Choose uplifting programs or a religious video rather than yielding to the constant bombardment of violence and sex which can dull the spirit and make viewers into cultural and spiritual zombies.

Psychologists tell us that a steady diet of bad TV has a detrimental effect on children. The same can be true for most of us during those times of illness, convalescence, or old age when we have neither the energy nor interest in constructive outlets.

3. Avail yourself of the Lord's healing sacraments.

Along with any medical therapy, dose yourself with three healing sacraments given by the Divine Physician:

The Sacrament of Reconciliation gives our souls and spirits the inner cleansing we need. In addition to ongoing private confession of our sins to God, there is a real assurance that we have been forgiven when a priest "stands in" for Christ. We all know that when we suffer there can be a spiritual compost heap within, an accumulation of bitterness and resentment that eats away at us. Doctors have known for a long time that such attitudes can actually trigger and perpetuate certain physical problems. On the other hand, the inner peace that one gets from confession can bring positive, healing chemical changes in the body.

The Sacrament of the Sick, once commonly referred to as "last rites," was for years a misunderstood channel of grace. At one time this sacrament was administered only to the dying, but since Vatican II the focus of the sacrament has reclaimed its original emphasis on healing. Through anointing with oil and prayer by the priest, as set forth in Scripture (see James 5:14-15), the sick person is often restored physically as well as spiritually. Unfortunately, it is not used as much as it probably should be for the handicapped, the elderly, or anyone about to undergo major surgery. When someone has a long and complex condition, they should ask a priest periodically for this sacrament. In addition, loved ones should be encouraged to amplify its effect by praying with the individual themselves in the days immediately following.

The Sacrament of Holy Communion, received either privately or during the eucharistic celebration, is undoubtedly the most powerful of the healing sacraments. After all, if Jesus really is "a life-giving spirit" (1 Cor 15:45) then it should come as no surprise that it is he himself in Holy Communion who can restore us. The early Christians certainly believed this, and their liturgies were more like healing services where people expected and then received all kinds of healing.

Though I once was blessed by physical healing when I received the sacrament while hospitalized, most of us have experienced the curative effects of this sacrament in small ways, such as becoming totally tranquil even after coming to church upset over something.

My healing came after weeks of being completely unable to swallow. I felt quite depressed, then early one Sunday morning, I was awakened by a replacement chaplain as he held a consecrated host before my face, saying softly, "Body of Christ."

Had he been there long? This young priest obviously didn't know my condition. Without thinking I closed my eyes, opened my mouth, and then simply, instinctively... I just swallowed. It was not until some minutes later I saw he had gone as wordlessly as he had come. It was then I realized with a racing heart what had happened. Jesus had healed me! This was amply verified soon after, when I was able to eat breakfast. Who was that chaplain who had never been around before—or later? Maybe my angel? I was too timid to ask, or even to tell the astounded nurses and doctors what really happened.

4. Offer it up!

It may seem like a theological platitude, but since much suffering is unavoidable anyway, it should be put to some specific spiritual good. A quick extemporaneous prayer will suffice, something like, "Heavenly Father, I offer you the uncomfortable treatment on my ulcerated leg today, in union with the offering of Jesus, your Son, for…" It could be for the soul of a relative, for children in the midst of war, for reconciliation in a friend's marriage, or any particular concern we have about the suffering of others.

Since we are not setting ourselves up as the sole object of anxiety, this is both spiritually and psychologically beneficial. We learn it is quite true that in giving we receive. As Bishop Fulton Sheen used to say, the problem with suffering is that it is "wasted" by so many people.

By the same token, it is not only wasteful but potentially harmful to offer up pain for the wrong reasons. We do not offer our pain to appease a tyrannical God who uses our suffering as punishment. Nor should one think offering it up is earning heaven. Above all, our offering up pain is not a fake spiritual cop-out that removes our responsibility—we have to cooperate in our own rehabilitation!

How does a simple prayer of offering actually work? It begins with acknowledging the fact that Jesus' sufferings on our behalf are of infinite value to the Father. These sufferings have an incredible power to gain God's favor and grace. So, when we unite our own sufferings, problems, perplexities, weakness, or frustration to those of his Son, they acquire a new and immense potential.

We create an indefatigable energizing force, one we can compare to a powerful magnifying glass. That magnifying glass—the offering of our Lord Jesus—picks up what we might consider our weak little offerings and magnifies them beyond our wildest expectations. It is not until we make a habit of doing this regularly that it becomes an eye-opener. We begin to see the unbelievable things which can happen to the persons or situations for which we offered up our pain. What a shame, indeed, to waste such potential!

The doctrine a person holds (consciously or unconsciously) may be a *result* of his temperament and life, but it also *shapes* his temperament and life...

There is no doctrine of life so conducive to the reestablishment and perfection of psychological equilibrium as that delivered by Christ to his Church.[1]

Raphael Simon O.C.S.O., M.D.
Hammer and Fire

FOUR

Sometimes I Can't Even Think

I do not cease to give thanks for you, remembering you in my prayers, that the God of our Lord Jesus Christ, the Father of glory, may give you a spirit of wisdom and of revelation in the knowledge of him, having the eyes of your hearts enlightened, that you may know what is the hope to which he has called you, what are the riches of his glorious inheritance in the saints, and what is the immeasurable greatness of his power in us who believe...

EPHESIANS 1:16-19

The July temperature was over one hundred degrees. An energetic fly probed my paralyzed toes. My right side was rigid and I had lost all equilibrium and coordination. In addition, double vision gave me two distinct images of myself in the mirror on the opposite wall.

As a twenty-seven-year-old multiple sclerotic wife and mother, I lay bathed in anger and discomfort—and extreme frustration. Pray? I wasn't even able to think—except to wonder which sad reflection caused by my faulty eyesight was really me. I tried to command a wooden arm, forgetting that, even if I could locate my head, there would still be two hands that reached up to two heads—separate ones.

"Augh! I know I have a head someplace!"

This was one of God's "teachable moments," but I flunked miserably! It goes without saying that there are times in our lives when we are so overwhelmed we certainly think that we cannot think anymore.

In reality, some kind of thought process goes on, albeit distorted or disoriented. Our brain waves continue in some form, even during comas or when we are anesthetized for surgery. Healing professionals are aware of this, and operating room doctors and nurses should bear in mind the potential harm of negative conversation.

What we really mean, therefore, when we say we can't think is that we are so stressed out or badgered with distractions that we are not thinking rationally or with as clear an awareness as before. The "self" we know is now impaired.

Setting Things Straight

There are any number of serious physical and/or psychological problems which make a person incapable of lucid thinking and appropriate behavior. These could involve drugs or a wide variety of physical difficulties.

Many drugs—both prescription and non-prescription—can make us feel we have lost our ability to think. (Flu sufferers can attest to that!) But even such ongoing medications as insulin and thyroid drugs, which can be taken for years with no adverse effect, sometimes make people stir-crazy if the dosage is not correct. There are also numerous nutritional deficiencies (such as certain members of the Vitamin B family) which can have a pronounced effect on the thinking process.

If there are exceptionally long periods when we feel as

though our heads were in a cement mixer—and we cannot find a logical cause—it may be God's way of telling us that it is time for professional counseling or an in-depth medical diagnosis. These, too, can be his tools for healing. To lose touch with reality is both spiritually and psychologically bad. As St. John of the Cross said, "The glory of God is man fully alive."[2]

The truth, however, is there are many people who are only three-quarters alive but who are trying to present a different facade. There is the young model who finds herself in bondage to "panic attacks," or the middle-aged woman with agoraphobia (the abnormal fear of public places) so severe she cannot leave her home. Even those who seem so "in control" on a professional level suffer secret personal pain, like the wealthy lawyer whose night terrors are so severe he has fallen out of bed and fractured bones—the breaks alleged to be "skiing accidents."

Many with excessively busy and demanding jobs find themselves mired in something of a temporary psychic paralysis. Other times the cause is just the opposite: insufficient stimuli, boredom, or feeling totally useless on any meaningful level. The danger here is of sinking into total self-absorption and stagnation. It is much like the old woman who sits, motionless, in a rocking chair, or the nursing home patient who stares blankly at one television show after another. Their thinking processes are hardly enhanced by such monofocal preoccupation with mindless distraction.

Many of the elderly and disabled are prone to this kind of dangerous "babysitting" in hospitals or rehabilitation centers. Unfortunately, this kind of inertia has a deadening effect on the mental processes, which in turn can cause hope to flicker and die out altogether.

This was proven to me once, while I was on one of my hospital "vacations." My three roommates were all around eighty, and, according to the morning nurse, interested in nothing.

"I really could use your help, ladies!" I said loudly from my bed, up in a sitting position, facing them all, "You're the right age for a seniors' musical I'm thinking of writing."

Two seemed so mesmerized by the TV it took a while for my words to register. The other lifted her white head and, supporting herself on one elbow, smiled weakly, "Want us to sing and dance or something?" Then in sad hopelessness, "We're too old..."

"We can just sing and sway in bed! I'm sure you all know 'Bicycle Built For Two' and 'Daisy'.... Are you with me? Let's try.... We've seen our doctors and had our meds. C'mon..."

By the time the stunned nurse on the next shift came in, the small cardiac ward was all sitting up, swaying and singing "oldies." We each held "flowers" we had made of colored tissues and straws, another bloom stuck in our hair. And the words to all the songs came back to the women, long-term memory no problem. They could think again! A mini-gift from God... however brief.

Apart from the causes associated with age and infirmity, nothing breaks down one's emotional and mental capacity as much as a festering residue of uselessness and unwantedness. This "emotional deficiency disease" is an Achilles heel for those who are chronically ill, and the devil uses this gradual process to wear down even the most sincere Christians.

The reason is quite simple. Unless our adult minds have been deliberately steered toward the possibility of hope in something, however small, we invariably yield to the quicksand of self-pity and hopelessness. We grow increasingly discouraged with our discouragement as we fearfully anticipate the worst.

Then, slowly and imperceptibly, all we have known of God and our faith fades into irrelevance and we end up utterly controlled by negative feelings. Somewhere in the depths of our hearts we may be aware of the black cloud that has enveloped us but, in a perverse sort of way, seems to provide comfort.

Trying to force ourselves to think positive thoughts—especially about God and his goodness—is next to impossible. Should a loved one or friend attempt to help by pointing out the error of our thoughts, it can be downright infuriating! So we end up swirling in an abyss of guilt and anger at that person, at God, and at ourselves.

Looking to the Light

Jesus, who is always true to his word, has promised that no sincere follower of his would ever be turned away. So we at least know the direction toward which we must take our first step if we are somehow to resurrect the virtue of hope in our lives. And it is vital that we understand how true the old adage, "hope springs eternal," actually is. Without hope, how can we trust God for anything?

In down-to-earth words, what makes hope possible? How can we set our thoughts to attaining it?

How can a devoted wife, bone weary from caring for her husband, a stroke victim, find hope when she herself has developed a painful back problem? What is hope to a family when one of its members with diabetes must have a leg amputated? Is hope merely a fantasy to the parents of a mentally-ill teenager who must be constantly monitored and medicated for violent episodes of schizophrenia?

Hope can only become operative if, in the depths of our hearts, we accept the incredible riches of our faith. As Scripture says, "By (God's) great mercy we have been born anew to a living hope through the resurrection of Jesus Christ from the dead" (1 Pt 1:3). The operative phrases here are "born anew" and "living hope"!

By virtue of our baptism we have been "absorbed" into Christ. As our love life with God is deepened and perfected through the years, moreover, a spiritual osmosis occurs. Eventually the Spirit awakens us to the fact that somehow Jesus is actually alive in us, that there is a special bonding. He cares about my cares and identifies with my pain. Even more important to understand on a practical level, it is his strength and his support which bear me up and supply that "living hope."

In order to grow in this awareness, however, we have no choice but to surrender our own plans and desires—no matter how necessary and good they may seem to us. Unless we allow God to take over and direct our lives, we will never glimpse his loving care and compassion. We will never understand his faithful, unchanging character.

Spiritual masters tell us that hope is actually rooted in memory. As we remember in some present difficulty how God's faithful love has come through in past situations, we begin to project a hope for the future. We may not know how God will work things out, but we are inwardly convinced that he most assuredly will bring good out of our stumbling efforts.

The stroke victim's wife, for instance, is less fearful when she reminds herself of all the help she received from friends when needing a knee replacement the previous year. The diabetic accepts the fact that life can go on, even with an artificial limb. In fact, his family recalls how, often before, he has met and grown through challenges. As for the parents of the schizophrenic son, they realize and admit that he has become far more faithful in taking his needed medication than before, and that he has begun developing a few healthy outside relationships.

Does such "hope memory" hold true even when events or people seem to have made our lives nothing but a mental blur? Absolutely!

We may be so mentally sluggish that we refuse to scan past events in our lives because, if we are at all honest, we must admit that bad things turned out at least "all right" and bearable—if not better. At this point, the devil will do his utmost to keep us from remembering such things. After all, we are told you can't prove that there will be any kind of change in the problem. Things look the same.

St. Paul knew all about such negative tactics, saying, "For in this hope we were saved. Now hope that is seen is not hope. For who hopes for what he sees? But if we hope for what we do not see, we wait for it with patience" (Rom 8:24-25).

Prayer for Inner Hope

Do not look forward to what might happen tomorrow.
The same everlasting Father... who cares for you today
Will take care of you... tomorrow and every day...
Either he will shield you from suffering,
Or he will give you unfailing strength to bear it.
Be at peace then and put aside
All anxious thoughts and imaginations.

St. Francis DeSales

Follow-up Action

1. What not to do!

If your head is spinning and you know your thinking is incoherent, do not badger yourself with self-condemnation. Do not try searching for a cause unless it is overwhelmingly obvious and calls for some immediate action (like putting all liquor, drugs, cigarettes, or medications out of sight to prevent both temptation and accidents).

2. "Crisis Day" schedule.

If possible, declare yourself a very personal on-the-spot vacation, a "24-hour goof-off day" when only those actions which are absolutely essential are considered. Alter and tone down routine tasks. Mostly, resolve not to make any big decisions.

3. First "medicate" your inner environment.

Dose yourself with spiritual affirmations three times daily. Repeat the following aloud five times each:

- The Lord is my shepherd. He restores my soul.
- I can do all things through Christ who strengthens me.
- His peace he gives. Peace is his gift to me.
- All things work for good to those who love the Lord.

4. Pray the rosary slowly (aloud, if possible, even if it does not appeal to you).

Multitudes of people, including theologians and psychologists, are (re)discovering the power of this traditional prayer/meditation in which we ask the Mother of God to intercede for us. After all, the pain and confusion she experienced beneath Jesus' cross qualifies her empathetic concern for the suffering of her spiritual children. The controlled repetition of prayers, moreover, becomes for many people something of a calming "mantra" in times of stress.

5. Bless yourself with holy water and pray:

"Jesus, keep me in the light of your love. Surround me with your holy angels. Cover my sins with your precious blood. Keep me

from all evil." (Holy water is a time-honored sacramental to break the hold of darkness.)

6. Address Satan simply:

"I am a child of God. You have no power over me. In the powerful name of Jesus Christ, I rebuke you. Leave me. Leave this room. Leave this house."

7. Then tell Jesus:

"Lord Jesus, you deal with any negative spirits according to your will. I place all my hope and trust in you. Flood me with your love... your peace... and your joy."

8. Immediately do something to distract yourself in a positive way.

For about an hour, play some uplifting or inspiring music. Call a good friend and chat. Do some gardening. Swing at a few golf balls. Do anything you find personally enjoyable.

9. Get your Bible and ask the Holy Spirit to open your mind and heart to these passages:

- Psalm 42—about the downcast soul, hoping in God
- 2 Corinthians 4:8—about not fixing our gaze on what is transitory
- Ephesians 6:10—on drawing strength from the Lord and his power

10. Ask the Spirit what you can do for someone else, something that is totally unexpected.

Phone a sick, house-bound relative. Bake a "reconciliation cake" for a person who hurt you or disappointed you in some way. Swallow your pride and write that overdue note of apology.

11. Attend to "clean-up" operations:

- Thank God for all his help, now and in the days to come.
- Deliberately choose not to think of the mental rut you were in.
- Make every effort to start the habit of positive thinking.
- Move on!

The very core of compassion is standing with others as equals, recognizing the other as brother or sister and being one with that person, especially in his or her struggles or sufferings... even when one cannot do for others, compassion impels one to be present... if only in silent presence, like Mary at the foot of the cross.[1]

William F. Hogan, C.S.C.
Spiritual Life

FIVE

Nobody Really Understands

Bless the Lord, O my soul,
> and forget not all his benefits,
who forgives all your iniquity,
> who heals all your diseases,
who redeems your life from the Pit,
> who crowns you with steadfast love and mercy.

PSALMS 103:2-4

"I could name so many things wrong with me, they could probably cover every letter in the alphabet," Lillian bemoaned that hot summer day. "Let's see...'A' for arthritis, 'B' for bursitis, 'C' for nervous colon, 'D' for double vision, 'E' for energy loss..."

"Heaven help us! Now you hush. Stop feeling sorry for yourself," chided Grandmama, an elderly Southern neighbor who had just popped in to visit the young teacher on health leave.

"Maybe you shouldn't have asked me how I was doing," was the sad reply.

"Well, since you can't read right now," the perky great grandmother went on, holding up a book, "I came over to share this."

Lillian braced herself inwardly, not knowing what kind of self-help advice Grandmama had brought over this time. Today it was about praising God for all things. As the older woman read slowly and with intonation, her eyes darted to Lillian as if to punctuate a special word or phrase—and she repeated the words if she detected no outward reaction.

"Stop!" Lillian suddenly blurted, surprising even herself. "This isn't helping... you're kind to come over and all, but you don't understand what my life is like. Nobody does."

Grandmama sat back and pushed up her bifocals, closing the book and studying her for an uncomfortable moment. "You say, Lillian, that nobody understands. That's true for everybody, my dear. Tell me, how much do you understand about losing your husband and raising five small children in the Depression? Do you have any idea what it is like to get them all up at night to search in the dirt for potatoes the farmers missed? Or to have two of your babies die in one year?"

"I didn't know... I'm sorry."

"Sooner or later, we learn one thing. God's the only one who really understands. Maybe doctors help. And people help. Only Jesus gives hope when things are downright hopeless!"

Many senior citizens remember a time when clergymen and doctors evoked the utmost respect from most people. Secrets of soul and body were freely and confidentially shared. In fact, the anticipated arrival of either a priest or family doctor (both of whom made house calls) meant that the house had to be squeaky clean. Children were drilled to respect privacy, and pets were shooed down into the basement.

Not so in today's world of computerized caring! While much can be said for relaxed relationships and more lay assertiveness, the basic need for humans to be understood in their life-problems remains unchanged. There is an instinctive yearning to receive personal compassion and empathy, be it a youngster stung by a wasp or a business executive who was informed he has a bladder malignancy—just two weeks after having been "downsized" out of a job.

The child has a great need for a mother's "cuddle-and-kiss" therapy. The executive has great inner needs too, primary being that he be treated as a *patient* (a time-accepted term always associated with someone who suffers) rather than merely a *client* (the recipient of medical services by business-oriented "providers").

Setting Things Straight

In essence, what we all reach for in times of physical, mental, or spiritual need is to be ministered to by someone who really cares for us personally. Though we may never articulate it, we have a vague hunger for at least one person—be it relative, friend, or doctor—with tenderness and gracious acceptance, who does not judge our faults and motives and whose ongoing love can be counted on.

Much too often we are disappointed. The underlying reason is that we are looking for God's kind of love, *agape* love, from others. Such pure love is beautifully described by "the great theophany," God's description of himself in the Old Testament (see Exodus 33:19, 34:5-7). It is more fully exemplified, of course, on the cross of Calvary. All his life, until Jesus handed over his spirit to the Father, he gave and forgave with perfect, selfless love—*agape* love. As for ourselves, when our instinctive hunger for *agape* love is not met, we often tend to perceive our situation from the standpoint of victimization.

It becomes the fault of others that we are not restored to health, to emotional well-being, to social or economic stability, etc.

Whether in word or in thought, we complain and grumble about not having had our need understood. If we hone in on a single individual or place of employment, for instance, a disastrous mental imbalance can result. This can erupt in the kind of job-related killings which are constantly in the media. If the blaming is generalized and remains merely verbal, then the targets are "the medical establishment," "those politicians," or "the church." The trouble is that eventually we run the risk of falling into a sea of spiritual glue. We become bitter, resentful, and unforgiving.

Creeping judgmentalism, seeming so justified at first, can put us into an emotional environment in which we become our own worst enemy. Continual blaming backfires. We may be oblivious to it, but there comes a time when we too are unable to give needed love to others—much less *agape* love. Should this be brought to our attention and we indignantly deny what is happening, our original problem is exacerbated and is actually perpetuated!

This negative progression has been part of the human scene ever since Eve blamed the snake and Adam blamed Eve for expulsion from Paradise. It is likely to continue for many millennia, unless there is divine intervention. In our own time, when secular humanism has replaced an estranged God, it is not even hard for many nominal Christians to think first of themselves and their own interests.

When rights are given top billing in our lives, the spirit gradually shrivels. We become spiritually myopic. We simply cannot grasp the suffering need in others. It should come as no surprise then that so few care to understand our suffering by listening with an open heart.

Looking to the Light

Incredible as it may seem, it is actually possible to have great inner peace in the midst of pain, perplexity, and all kinds of discomfort. By shifting our focus, we can discover ourselves completely understood by a caring God who "loves us into accepting" whatever deprivation or trouble besets us each day.

In all this we are, as St. Paul says, "more than conquerors" (Rom 8:37). While we are barred by circumstances from many things—ease, economic security, excellent health—still there is nothing in this world or the next that can separate us from the love of God which is ours through his Divine Son, our Lord Jesus Christ.

Pie in the sky?

Is this too religious to make sense for modern believers, especially when we wear ourselves out trying to cope with suffering that seems unending? Or when we give up hoping for the compassionate and loving care we crave? Not so. Being a "conqueror" does not require climbing a mountain on one's knees. Nor accepting the dismal conclusion that just because the vast majority of people do not give God's perfect kind of love right now they cannot give some love that is quite beneficial.

To be a "conqueror" requires only that we act on two powerful spiritual principles, *giving* and *forgiving*. This is especially true of people who must live with disabling, chronic pain, slow but steady, that cannot be treated surgically and that goes on and on for months and even years. In some cases, as doctors know, it is possible to modify the pain which reaches the individual's brain through the dorsal horn or "gate" in the spinal column. How can this happen?

Psychologists tell us that if we resolve to superimpose other strong thoughts over "pain thoughts" there is less pain. The brain simply processes less pain when we deliberately choose to dwell on something "higher." We may be suffering an excruciating headache, for instance, but it is immediately put on hold if we see a small child chasing a ball in front of a moving car. Instinctively, we run out and grab him, forgetting ourselves. We choose to shift priorities.

Superimposed spiritual thoughts which have become a habit—turning to Jesus or the Blessed Mother, believing that with God "all things are possible," and thanking him for some past blessings—are truly effective in lessening pain. It is a fact that people who find more things sacred and who cling to a definite purpose and meaning in life report less pain and less panic. This was the result of a recent pain management study at West Virginia University Hospital.

"Research shows active believers who develop a personal faith are better able to withstand a crisis when it comes along," says Fr. Joseph Hayden, S.J., psychology professor.[2]

The Giving Principle

Those who are willing can be led by the Spirit to act on the powerful "giving principle." This means that we deliberately *choose* to forget our own needs and concentrate on the problems of others—*for the time being*. For example, in the midst of our own need for compassionate understanding, we give an understanding ear to the family whose home was destroyed by a fire. We weep with the wife who has had three miscarriages and now has a tubal pregnancy. We pray with a friend, asking Jesus to touch his wayward son as he touched the Apostle Paul on Damascus Road (see Acts 9:1-9).

When we put ourselves aside and reach out like this, we tap into the secret of divine supply. God has promised that it is in giving that we receive. And this truth can be proven.

We need not worry about scraping the bottom of our spiritual barrel and simply running out of the strength to give. The reason—in the logic of the Almighty—is that in proportion to our own degree of generosity, God will supply his abundant grace. Each day he will "restock" whatever blessings or spiritual gifts we need. Then, when we are afraid of hitting "empty," our hope in him begins to ease our weariness and we can go on one day at a time.

Certainly there will be times of doubt. The devil constantly works to manipulate us with the rationalization "You really ought to look out only for yourself!" Of course we must assure reasonable care of ourselves, taking advantage of both medical means and prayer. The more we practice God's giving principle, however, the more we allow room for God to do his work of healing in us!

The Forgiving Principle

Many of us, however, simply cannot do this. We may find it virtually impossible to give unless the Holy Spirit first makes us aware of all the unforgiveness that is clogging our hearts. After all, few of us are immune to "love deficiency disease"! Our hurts may be very deep, or even unconsciously repressed, but we still hold on to them like a cracked walking stick!

The "stick" of self-justified resentment simply cannot support us. It is a powerful spiritual poison which blocks the flow of life and healing. At the same time, it prevents us from following the forgiving principle. Because we cannot forgive from the heart, as Our Lord asks, any hope that our own needs will be met simply fades like a morning mist.

Genuine forgiveness can be very hard, more so when the

person causing our pain has died. Likewise, it can be intimidating beyond words to ask someone for forgiveness. In both instances, we must stand humbly at the foot of Christ's cross. In the very depths of our hearts we must consider the immense love of this God/man before us.

The horrific scene presents One whose face was streaked with the blood of the thorny crown, whose back leaned in blistering pain from a cruel scourging, and whose hands and feet were immovably suspended in stabbing pain. We listen closely. We hear his clear words directed to Heaven through deep, indrawn breaths, "Father forgive them; for they know not what they do" (Luke 23:34).

The Prayer of St. Francis

Lord, make me an instrument of your peace.
Where there is hatred let me sow your love,
Where there is injury, pardon,
Where there is doubt, faith,
Where there is despair, hope,
Where there is darkness, light,
And where there is sadness, joy.
O Divine Master, grant that I may not so much seek
To be consoled as to console,
To be understood as to understand,
To be loved as to love,
For it is in giving that we receive,
It is in pardoning that we are pardoned,
And it is in dying that we are born to eternal life.

St. Francis of Assisi

Follow-up Action

1. Repeat the Our Father very slowly.

Spend at least five minutes reflecting on what could well be termed a "dangerous" prayer. After all, we ask God to forgive our sins in the same way that we forgive others who have offended us—slowly? begrudgingly?

2. Pray to the Holy Spirit:

"Lord, you are the Giver of Life. Jesus has said that you are my Helper, my Consoler, my Counselor, and my Guide. I need your help in order to forgive. I cannot do it alone. The anger and resentment I feel inside are eating me up like a cancer."

3. Jot down any good things you know about this person.

Our feeling of bitterness has probably prevented us from being able to see the positive side, but there really must be something good. If this is difficult, ask the Spirit to reveal those positive things to you—even if it takes the rest of the day, you cannot skip this!

4. Ask God to show you what the person's motive was in doing the upsetting things.

Was it a deliberate attempt to hurt? Could we have somehow provoked what happened? Under the same circumstances, if our roles were reversed, would we have done any differently? (This is especially important with parents who did the best they knew how or sincerely considered that their action was for their child's best interests.)

5. Write down the specific things you have against this person.

We must take our time, asking for grace to be brutally honest.

6. Read and meditate on the following Scripture passages:

- Luke 6:27-38 (the Golden Rule) and 41-43 (about fault-finding in others)
- Romans 2:1 (on self-conviction through judging others)
- Colossians 3:12-15 (what the behavior of God's chosen ones must be)

7. Imagine Jesus suddenly appearing right before us.

In the light of these three readings, could we explain the wrong which we think was done to us without any hesitation or shame? If the Spirit brings to mind any way in which we were guilty of wronging anyone, this too must be noted.

8. Pray sincerely for the gift to forgive and the gift to love.

Based on what we have written, and on any other inner revelations of the Spirit, we might pray like this:

Heavenly Father, I come before you with a changed and contrite heart.
I see the barriers I have placed around this heart.
I confess to smoldering resentment and self-pity over what was done to me
while being blind to the hurts and wrongs which I caused others.
In the Name of Jesus, Abba, I ask your warming love to melt away those barriers.
Give me the courage and strength to change my ways
Take a portion of the love which you have for the one who hurt me...

and give it to me. Then we will love him together.
Jesus, My Lord and my God, I thank you for showing the path
  of forgiveness.
You have died so I might truly live!
You have set me free!

9. Make a firm personal decision that you will do your part to imitate Jesus' "giving heart."

This is most effective once we are sure that all efforts have been made to forgive, even if it is "seventy times seven times," as Jesus taught. It is work, because we must *will* to let his grace make it a habit for us. We can be sure we are on the right course when the one forgiven no longer triggers bitterness or resentment—even if he or she is unaware of that forgiveness. As St. Catherine of Siena concluded, there exists only one thing of value that we are in a position to offer God, and that is to give God's love to people who are no more worthy of it than we are.

10. Stand your guard against the slippery sin of self-righteousness.

After we have diligently put aside our hurts and forgiven others, after we have begun to give in whatever small way possible (maybe only a sincere smile) and after we have begun to feel that wonderful inner peace, the devil often tries a different tactic. He tries to make us proud of our humility; he tempts us to believe that our goodness now far surpasses that of others. To one's life of faith this is as poisonous a venom as unforgiveness. So for balanced spiritual health, disregard any kind of comparisons and keep your eyes on Jesus!

We need to tell the disabled what they can do, not what they can't do, and help them to set and pursue realistic goals...[1]

Ellen Burstein, spokeswoman for
"assisted living, not assisted dying," author of
Legwork: An Inspiring Journey Through a Chronic Illness

SIX

What Good Am I to Anyone?

O God, from my youth thou hast taught me,
and I still proclaim thy wondrous deeds.
So even to old age and grey hairs,
O God, do not forsake me,
till I proclaim thy might to all the generations to come...
thou who hast made me see many sore troubles wilt revive
me again.

PSALMS 71:17-18, 20

"How can I have a birthday if I wasn't born?" the vivacious, blue-eyed teenager teased her adoptive mother, right after guessing correctly that she must have been the result of an unsuccessful abortion. Discovering that would have a vital impact on her and on many other young people.

Giana Jessen's birth-mother was well into her sixth month of pregnancy when she was given a toxic salt solution. Instead of an aborted fetus, however, she delivered a two-pound baby girl—one who would have problems galore. The loss of oxygen during the abortion caused cerebral palsy and spina bifida.

Doctors did not expect her to live, much less ever be able to sit or walk.

She proved them all wrong. At three-and-a-half years of age—the day her adoption was finalized—spunky little Giana, with her swinging golden pigtails, was able to dress herself, tie her shoes, and even walk out the door unassisted! Who would have predicted that there was much more to come—that ten years later, after many adjustments, operations, therapy sessions, and clumsy braces, she would sing and dance into the hearts of thousands of people across this country and abroad as well!

Giana Jessen is now a talented, bubbling missionary for life. Her pro-life presentations evoke a great many letters from other teenagers who thank her for giving them hope or who tell of having their minds changed about getting an abortion.[2]

But what if she and her adoptive parents had not kept up hope and had not worked so hard at her rehabilitation? Suppose she had remained virtually powerless and totally dependent? Would she have had any less value as a member of the human family? Surely not in God's estimation. Far from it.

As for modern society, there has been a radical reversal concerning the "worth" of an individual. This applies not only to the handicapped and other non-productive people, but to the homeless and elderly as well. People seem so preoccupied with themselves they seldom identify with such needs. As one rabbi pointed out, "the opposite of life is not death but insensitivity."

People on the fringes are appraised as having lives without the proper "quality" and, therefore, lives not really worth much. It is a short step then from devaluing people to finding expedient ways to eliminate them. In Hitler's Germany it was not the racially or ideologically unwanted who were the first to go, but the "useless eaters." Dr. Leo Alexander has observed this country is following the same trend toward the non-rehabilitative sick.[3]

Setting Things Straight

In our escalating "culture of death" we are indeed plummeting down "the slippery slope" begun with legalized abortion. Unlike abortion, however, sooner or later everyone is bound to be affected personally by the cheapening of life.

For this reason it is extremely important that we do some sincere introspection, that we search our hearts and admit to ourselves what we honestly believe about all this. Do we consider ourselves useless in times of suffering because we cannot contribute in a meaningful way? Do we speak and act exactly like a person without faith? When we see a serious but curable illness, or even one which the doctors say will be fatal, have we adopted the utilitarian equation:

Personal Worth=Capability to Function Normally

We must stop! Beginning with ourselves, we must insist that every single human being, in whatever condition, has a value beyond price. Each of us is the personal property of God!

Certainly we can all attest to the fact that we may not feel such a lofty worth many times. This is especially true in prolonged suffering, when our whole awareness is that of being powerless, when we cannot wash or dress or even feed ourselves.

God knows something, however, that our minds are too bogged down to realize. In the midst of all we are enduring, he sees that we may be accomplishing more for his mysterious purposes than if we were physically capable and mentally alert! Over and over, therefore, we need to remind ourselves that it is not what we can do which matters most to God, but what we *are*. He made mankind the pinnacle of his creation. Herein lies our worth.

Nobody says it is easy to keep thinking like this, geared as we are to judge everything by feelings and appearances. Even a bad head cold can make us feel utterly useless. How much more a crippling illness or permanent injuries resulting from an accident?

Fears take over and revolve like a broken record in our brains: "If I take one more sick day for this asthma, I'll lose my job"; or "This cellulitis just keeps hanging on... it'll never heal!"; and "This lump I found is probably cancerous."

Erich Fromm has termed such thoughts "journeys which lead toward destruction," and they must be ended quickly. Conversely, the more we affirm and expect positive things, the less is the destruction of hopelessness. We can put this in a capsuled perspective with the poetic story of two men, convicts behind prison bars. As they walked down the hall they each stopped briefly to look out a barred window. One saw mud. The other saw stars.

We control our perspective by controlling where we look, whether to God and his purposes or to our pains and discouragements.

Looking to the Light

All of us have a God-given instinct to accomplish things and to be productive in this world. This is what impels human beings to achieve incredible feats of body and mind. And it applies to the spiritual life as well.

As Christians, our life on earth was not meant to be static. We were created and then redeemed to move on in Christ; made so we would do our part in establishing the coming Kingdom of God—however diverse our paths and methods of doing so, and however limited we may be by age or physical condition, or giftedness.

In the familiar parable of the laborers in the vineyard, Jesus illustrates God's call to service (see Matthew 20:1-16). Four times during the day the landowner went to the marketplace to hire workers. Finally, at five o'clock, when he still found idle workers milling around, he said, "You also go into the vineyard."

There is a presupposition here which must be understood: We must, like those workers, believe the One who calls us, and we must be willing to accept his conditions and his terms of payment for our work.

The different hours of the day in this gospel story can be compared to the various stages of a person's life. "One is led to a holy life during childhood, another in adolescence, another in adulthood, and another in old age," as St. Gregory the Great observed. To this we might add, "and many others are led during periods of sickness and seeming uselessness."

What happens when all discernible possibilities of working in God's "vineyard" diminish or seem to vanish altogether? What if God chooses that we serve only as inactive members of his body? How do we overcome the inner rebellion as our independence is threatened? Do we still prefer to accomplish things only on our own steam, even to our spiritual detriment?

All too often independence is an illusion we cling to with slippery hands. Take the man who is homebound for many months following near-fatal intestinal surgery. He steadfastly refuses to have Holy Communion brought to him either by his priest or a lay minister of the Eucharist, saying, "I'll never receive if I can't stand up on my own two feet to get it." In cases like this, when we are motivated by an inordinate sense of independence, there is always the danger of pride. The end result is that we cling to a false notion of independence, growing angry and bitter with every failure to achieve something.

Actually, the stark reality is that nobody is ever totally

independent. How could we be when all of creation would sink into black oblivion if it were not for the will and constant care of a loving God?

The way to become aware of this, to become a whole person within, is to operate on *interdependence*. This is the third option. It is beyond being either dependent or independent. It is the truer assessment of our reality and its possibilities. Once we decide to "let go" (of all we were once capable of doing alone, with efficiency and speed) and "let God" (allowing him to do his will in us, in his way, and in his time), the results can be quite amazing.

We find that while allowing ourselves to become as inert and lifeless as a pencil in the Divine Hand, we can still be mightily productive. It is in such yielding and offering up of our powerlessness that spiritual energy is generated, freeing God so it can be applied for his purposes. Two examples of this are found in the life of Louis Martin (the father of St. Thérèse of Lisieux) and in Mother Teresa's corps of disabled co-workers.

Martin, currently a candidate for canonization, was so grateful to God for all his blessings that, out of love for the human family, he told the Lord that whatever suffering lay in his future he would like applied to souls in purgatory. Very soon after, he had a series of strokes which left him disabled and senile. Only in heaven was he to learn the effects of his spiritual generosity.[4]

Mother Teresa, the Nobel Prize winner whose work is acclaimed worldwide, credits thousands of handicapped and incurably ill people with the success of her mission. They form a silent army of pray-ers, with one "sufferer" interceding and offering up each day for one specific active sister somewhere in the world. She says active nuns are like Martha in Scripture, and those who are ill and disabled are like Mary, sitting in rapt attention at the feet of Jesus.[5]

There comes a time, eventually, when all the giving seems too much. Still, as the noted American contemplative, Fr. M. Basil Pennington, puts it, "As long as we are living in Christ, we each have our role. If nothing else, just by being a living vital cell of the Body we help the whole to be healthy and vital."[6]

How can we remain that "living vital cell"? Through love, the very special, personal love of Jesus within our being. It is really so simple, so undemanding... yet so very assuring. It makes us smile. It lights up our eyes. It gives Christ's peace. This undiluted love has the power to touch all whom we encounter. It can change their lives. It can move mountains!

Lord, You Know...

Loving Lord, you are a reasonable God;
my hope in you goes on.
You do not expect the impossible from us.
You do not ask a child to gather in the harvest,
Nor an old man to break records in youthful competition.
You know our limitations, and you know our possibilities,
For you have fixed them with tender, loving care.

But Lord, you know too the successes sketched in your
great plan.
So you hold out your vision and await our "yes."
For you alone know the distance your strength can carry us,
And you alone know the pattern you have designed
for the beautiful tapestry of our lives.
To us it seems but a confusion of dangling strings,
But in Eternity, you will gladly show to us
the picture on the other side.

Follow-up Action

1. Compile a personal "Litany of Thanksgiving."

Ask the Holy Spirit to help you recall and be thankful for all that you were capable of doing and things which you have accomplished in the past. Write in a small notebook everything from being able to run after your children to your artistic talents. Take time. Be genuine. This is more than mere nostalgia.

2. Whenever a sense of uselessness threatens, pray after each line in your "litany":

"For this gift, I thank you, my Lord."

3. Re-evaluate your present capabilities.

Again, pray to the Spirit to help you with something like a "Works Inventory." Resist any temptation to dwell on what you are not able to do anymore and concentrate on what is still functioning. (Jotting it down really helps the memory.) Then, as I used to tell my growing sons, "Keep your eyes right on the donut and not on the hole!" "Yeah, Mom! You can't lose," was the rejoinder. "They even sell the holes!"

4. Become a reasonable "Risk Taker" for God!

There is much truth to the old adage, "If you don't use it, you lose it!"

Likewise, to grow in hope and trust of God's help, we must sometimes step out in faith by doing something hard, something we might have given up on. Pray for his assistance... believe he heard... then try! (But also pray to know when not to try.)

5. Consider time a gift from God. Never waste it on self-pity.

Even though it may seem justified by our problems, feeling sorry for ourselves day in and day out is really self-defeating. We dig a psychological hole which nobody wants to share with us. This is the biggest reason for falling back into the "I can't..." syndrome. A combination of self-pity and verbalizing constantly "I can't..." achieves only one thing—sooner or later it becomes a self-fulfilling prophesy!

6. Find new ways of doing old things.

Whether we expect to be incapacitated for months or even years, we need imagination and creativity to get around the way something used to be done. Feel left out of the mainstream of society? Write letters to the editor. Can't leave the house because of stairs? Try going down backwards, holding a rail with each hand, as my physical therapist taught me. Feeling frustrated because you miss teaching? How about tutoring on the phone or by computer?

7. Turn mere chatting into power.

If there are friends or neighbors who visit regularly—and who share spiritual interests—why not finish the coffee time with intercessory prayer? Instead of reciting your symptoms and problems as an update, why not ask that you all say a simple prayer instead? Then broaden it to include the needs of others.

(For years there was such a regular Wednesday gathering at our house which attracted both Catholics and other Christians just by word of mouth.)

8. Start a phone prayer chain in your parish.

One or two friends plus a notice in the bulletin can begin a list of parishioners willing to pray for the serious needs of fellow parishioners, their families, and friends. No fuss. No meetings. This is a spiritual outreach which requires only a single person to receive calls and start the chain—and the prayer chain is usually welcomed by pastors as a community builder.

I fled him down the nights and down the days; I fled him, down the arches of the years... down the labyrinthine ways of my own mind; and in the mist of tears I hid from him... adown titanic glooms of chasméd fears...

Yet ever and anon a trumpet sounds
From the hid battlements of eternity...
"Rise, clasp my hand and come!"[1]

Francis Thompson
The Hound of Heaven

SEVEN

I'm So Lonely...
So Sad...
So Afraid

Peace I leave with you; my peace I give to you; not as the world gives do I give to you. Let not your hearts be troubled, neither let them be afraid... As the Father has loved me, so I have loved you; abide in my love. If you keep my commandments, you will abide in my love, just as I have kept my Father's commandments and abide in his love. These things I have spoken to you, that my joy may be in you, and that your joy may be full.

JOHN 14:27; 15:9-11

There is a story of hope by Jaris Bragin that is both poignant and amusing.

"An old retired professor of church history at Yale is best remembered for the last words he ever spoke. He was on his deathbed. Waiting relatives anxiously gathered around him.

"After a time of silence one man quietly said, 'I think he's gone.'

"Another relative standing at the end of the bed felt the old man's feet and said, 'No, his feet are still warm. No one ever dies with warm feet.'

"The eyes of the old professor blinked open. He raised his head up from the bed and looked around at his family. 'Joan of Arc did!' he whispered. He gave a little chuckle and died."[2]

We can only surmise that a person who was able to literally end his life laughing had great inner peace, the kind of peace that only Christ can give. It is quite different from the end of political hostility or the termination of a physical attack from without. It is even different from the end of some verbal confrontation which has left us emotionally wounded.

Our present culture is a great anti-peace breeding ground. There are ubiquitous little wars both without and within, and merely watching the nightly news—with its usual menu of violence, conflict, distrust, and greed—can erode our joy and sense of well-being. It most certainly can rob us of trust in fellow human beings. So many of us "wall up," both literally and figuratively, keeping a safe emotional as well as physical distance from everyone and everything. Is it any wonder then that hope becomes dim and finally flickers out?

Such self-induced isolation, however, begins to feed on itself. It makes us feel lonely and sad. We find ourselves increasingly overwhelmed by fear and distress, and we find it just about impossible to agree with the psalmist who says, "This is the day which the Lord has made; let us rejoice and be glad in it" (Ps 118:24). Since we find little to rejoice in, we get a suspicious outlook on life and grow progressively more depressed.

"Why should I bother getting up in the morning?" the fifty-plus bachelor said soon after doctors diagnosed a growing arterial problem. "There's nothing to get up for!"

Such depression has been termed our "national epidemic"

by some social observers. It is an epidemic, however, which can be reversed by a simple remedy noted 3,000 years ago in the Old Testament: "A cheerful heart is a good medicine, but a downcast spirit dries up the bones" (Prv 17:22).

In recent decades both medicine and religion are rediscovering *joy* as an antidote to depression. It was found, for example, that joyfulness—along with love, hope, faith, a will to live, purpose, and determination—make a very profound difference in recovering from serious illness. Also, spontaneous eruptions of laughter can actually be a form of therapy.

The famed medical author, Norman Cousins, along with the prestigious UCLA Medical School, did prolonged empirical studies on the medical value of "the laughter connection." The book *Anatomy of an Illness* was written by Cousins to document his own bout with a nearly incurable disease which involved all the connective tissues of his body. It left almost unbearable inflammation of the spine and joints. His therapy was mega doses of Vitamin C along with "scheduled laughter" two hours each day—achieved by committing family and nurses to read joke books and by watching funny movies.[3]

Setting Things Straight

Father Denny Heck, an old ethics professor of mine, had laughed so much all his life that deep laugh lines remained on his face even when he was involved in a serious discussion. I remember well some of those "discussions" which he continued after class, walking right along with me clear across campus—never managing one simple frown!

One is drawn like a magnet to someone who bubbles over with inner joy and the peace of Christ. Audible laughter may be the effect, but not necessarily so. Inner joy radiates on our faces. Parenthetically, it is interesting to note, according to doctors, that fewer muscles are used when we smile than when we grimace or scowl.

Though smiles and laughter are good, inner joy runs deeper. If a funny joke catches us off-guard when we are in a depressive mood, it can sometimes jar the emotion. But unless we pursue further positive thoughts, we can sink right back into the doldrums. True joy, on the other hand, is the product of inner peace and remains steady. It can certainly rise in a ludicrous situation or when we are told a really hilarious story, but then all returns to the common denominator of a joyful heart.

It is the habit of being joyless that often needs to be broken. A few good belly laughs can often break the hold of hopelessness temporarily, most especially if we can laugh at ourselves! The more we can detect funny situations in our lives—no matter how others might view them—the less we tend to sink into the muck of gloom and self-pity.

One of many such times in my life came in the middle of the night when I woke my husband with, "Hon, I can't move..."

"Huh...?" he mumbled sleepily.

"...and I've got to go."

In an instant he got me up, put my hands around his neck and started to drag me into the bathroom, as he'd done other times when my legs were paralyzed. Now, however, my toes got stuck on the door sill as he pulled my upper torso. "Pick up your feet!" he called over his shoulder. My reply, "How...?" was so ironic that it can bring a laugh many years later when I recall our dilemma.

"Cultivate a sense of humor. Laughter is good medicine, and has always been good medicine," said Dr. Donald L. Cooper, a member of the President's Council on Physical Fitness, who himself battled depression at one time. "My number one emphasis on managing stress is laughter," he advised, and among other things, "keep the faith."[4]

There are some hospitals that are receiving remarkable results from "laugh rooms" for chronically ill or "worn out" patients. Being exposed to humorous books, magazines, and movies, the patients not only begin to laugh themselves but benefit fellow patients by retelling something funny. Similarly, music therapy as well as clown therapy also evoke happy moods, especially in those children who are terminally ill.

There is also the Fellowship of Merry Christians, headed by Cal Samra, author of the book *The Joyful Christ: The Healing Power of Humor.*

A former director of the Huxley Institute, a psychiatric research foundation, Dr. Samra candidly credits Christ for healing him from crippling depression. It began when he encountered "merry-hearted priests and nuns with a keen sense of humor."[5] When Jesus tells us in the Bible, "Ask, and you will receive, that your joy may be full" (Jn 16:24), he makes it clear that we choose God's joy and claim it for our own. Every moment of every day we are given a chance to pick either cynicism or joy in each thought, word, or action.

"Increasingly, I am aware of all these possible choices, and increasingly I discover that every choice for joy in turn reveals more joy and offers more reason to make life a true celebration in the house of the Father," Henri Nouwen writes.[6]

What if we feel incapable of breaking through our lonely and fear-wracked sadness? What if we honestly believe that the cross(es) we have been given in life prevent us from choosing joy or laughter?

Laughing at ourselves can be the most difficult thing of all. Like the time I tried seriously listing all my just-verified allergies to a seminarian friend. By the time I got to #16, "camels," the compassionate look on his face crumpled into guffaws of laughter.

What we must both understand and accept is the fact that being joyful, as Jesus promised, does not deny our suffering and pain. Instead, it overcomes the distress because we 1) discover joy in the midst of our woundedness, 2) make a decision to claim it, and 3) act on that choice.

It is much like operating a video camera, decidedly moving from a scene of ugliness in the viewfinder of our mind and "discovering" one of beauty. By filming the latter we "claim" the positive picture. When the video is seen later on the TV monitor of our memory, it proves that our choice was "acted on." We preferred to look at the positive.

"I praise and thank God that I had my stroke at forty," a laughing friend once told me, "because now that I am fifty I can benefit from all my nutty perseverance then... having to re-learn so much... getting use of my limbs again."

That friend is living proof of something that psychological research is now finding, that while a tendency to be unhappy may be in our genes, our capacity for joy is largely developed by ourselves. One of the problems in claiming and thereby enlarging our "joy box" is that we look for joy as though expecting an elephant. We want the big spectacular joys and miss the hidden and scarcely noticeable ones all around. We look for a forest but never notice the intricate and beautiful plan in a single leaf. In this, we are lucky indeed that our expectations are not God's. He rejoices over the small, the forgotten, the insignificant evidence that one of his precious children has found him. As Fr. Nouwen writes, "From God's perspective, one hidden act of repentance, one little gesture of selfless love, one moment of true forgiveness is all that is needed to bring God from his throne to run to his returning son and to fill the heavens with the sounds of divine joy."[7]

There is still another dimension to all this, the effect which our joy—or grim lack of it—can have on others who are close to us. Just as one person's cough can trigger many "sympathy coughs" in a group (ideo-motor activity), our moods can also prove contagious. Our joy can grow and spread, infecting others with newfound hope.

"Just seeing someone express an emotion can evoke that mood in you," according to Dr. Ellen Sullins. "The dance of moods goes on between people all the time."[8]

Looking to the Light

In his priestly prayer after the Last Supper, Jesus asked the Father to protect his disciples. "While I was with them, I kept them in thy name, which thou hast given me," he said. "But now I am coming to thee; and these things I speak in the world, that they may have my joy fulfilled in themselves." (Jn 17:12, 13). Long before the sun would rise again, that joy of Jesus' would be eclipsed by sudden fear and great distress.

It is during the night, in the Garden of Gethsemane, that we usually identify most closely with him. It is here that he experiences the kind of powerlessness that we know so well. But we must not stop our meditation there, as though we have been dumped into a dark, shapeless void.

We are still with Jesus, the giver of hope. With him we must repeatedly pray that the Father's will be done, not ours. Thus, when our fear is accepted and united with Jesus' own fear, we begin to experience perfect love—which banishes all fear (see 1 John 4:18). The horrendous sense of loneliness recedes from the present moment and we are not chained to the terror of anticipating what lies ahead. However dimly, a pilot light of inner joy still burns in the most vital part of our being. So it was with Jesus.

This joy remained with him until his final words on the

cross. Yes, he felt utterly abandoned in his agony, repeating with the psalmist, "My God, my God, why hast thou forsaken me?" (Mt 27:46). Yet, he knew beyond the shadow of a doubt that his spirit would be accepted in love by the loving Father whose commandments he had kept so carefully.

Just like Jesus, the only thing we can know with absolute certainty is that God's kind of love will never end. Every other thing which brings pain to us in this world will pass away; in fact all things are passing except God, as St. Teresa of Avila always put it.

"The greatest honor you can give God," according to the fourteenth century mystic Julian of Norwich, "is to live gladly because of the knowledge of his love."

This pertains not only to those who are Christian, but to all people who believe in God as Supreme Being. This was exemplified in 1943 by Etty Hillesum, a Jewish woman who was killed in Auschwitz.

"I am deeply grateful to you, Oh God, for leaving me so free of bitterness and hate, with so much calm acceptance which is not the same as defeatism," she wrote in her diary, to be published later as the book *An Interrupted Life*. "They are merciless towards us, totally without pity. And we must be all the more merciful ourselves.... I know that a new and kinder day will come. I would so much like to live on, if only to express all the love I carry within me."[9]

To a far lesser degree, we are all given spiritual challenges by which to grow in trust. Can we mute all the many voices of doom and fear all around us, however, and still affirm that God loves us and will bring us through? Even when everything about us seems to be caving in, can we still cling to a personal hope?

O, Eternal Father,
Whose Infinite Love watches in Wisdom
over each day of my life,
grant me the light
to see in sorrow as in joy,
in trial as in peace,
in uncertainty as in confidence,
the way Your Divine Providence
has marked for me.

Give me that faith and trust
in Your care for me,
so pleasing to You
in St. Therese of the Child Jesus,
and I will walk in darkness
as in light,
holding Your hand and finding
in all the blessings I receive
from Your loving bounty, that
"Everything is a grace".

Carmel of Terre Haute

Follow-up Action

1. Begin each day with the Eucharist, if possible.

It is vital that the mind and soul begin each day focused on God. Because prisoners of loneliness and depression find it particularly hard not to dwell on themselves almost exclusively, spiritual help is needed. If we receive communion (even a spiritual communion via the TV Mass) we are far more capable of coping with the rest of the day. Reading from Scripture or the Divine Office is valuable too.

2. Make a habit of continually repeating:

"The joy of the Lord is [my] strength" (Neh 8:10). Quote this morning, noon, and night. Experience this prayer until it becomes a part of you and floods your subconscious mind. This is especially important if depression clings like a heavy, wet beach blanket.

"I have seen the spirit of depression vanish from many people when they prayed this prayer continually," says Fr. George DePrizio, retreat leader and hospital chaplain.[10]

3. Use the healing power of sacred music.

While almost anything from Gregorian chant to contemporary Christian rock can help dispel depression, many people find spiritual stimulation and joy in traditional hymns or "praise" songs. With recorded music, I personally find it easy to "pray twice," as St. Augustine put it, by singing along.

4. If circumstances permit, make a weekend retreat.

Of itself, this may not be a total answer to sadness, fear, and depression, but it may halt their progression. "I've known many people who were delivered of their depression and had their lives dramatically turned around in monastic or retreat center settings after psychiatrists or psychologists had failed to help them," says Cal Samra. "Others have been delivered from depression simply by becoming involved in prayer groups."[11]

5. Search out serious Christian fellowship, a spiritual "support system" or group.

Many people have benefited from Marriage Encounter, the Cursillo Movement, and Charismatic Renewal. The latter is the largest worldwide modern lay group approved by the hierarchy. Any archdiocesan chancery can give locations and times of parish prayer meetings. In addition, there are often larger healing services conducted by priests, as well as regional charismatic conferences.[12]

6. Consider an in-depth "healing of memories."

The subconscious mind is like a perpetually running tape recorder. From our mother's womb it has recorded every pleasure, pain, joy, sadness, distress, achievement, disappointment, and frustration. It is here that most of our emotional, psychological—and even spiritual—problems originate. The stark pain may have been lessened through counseling, prayer, and maturity but there is often something which was so overwhelming that it flashes on the screens of our mind almost daily. As one man put it, "If I live to be ninety-nine years old, I'll never forget how my father walked out on us."

In many charismatic prayer groups there is a special "healing of memories" before people are prayed over for a greater infilling of the Holy Spirit and his charisms or gifts. The leader, usually a priest, leads people through various phases of life—childhood, adolescence, pre-marriage, professional, and so forth—highlighting usual crisis points and praying for all the negative things to be healed by Jesus.

Scripture is taken quite literally when it says that "Jesus is the same yesterday and today and for ever"(Heb 13:8). In other words, he and his caring love exist out of time and are not restricted. He can easily move into our past and can do there what we can never do—simply remake it. All the painful events and people are not eliminated, as though none of this ever happened. Instead, through "faith imagination" we see Jesus entering into the picture, flooding our minds and hearts with a new awareness, understanding, and forgiveness. It is possible also to "pray through" our lives privately for such healing of memories. We ask the Spirit (generally before confession and communion) to reveal our hurts, the pain we may have caused others, any great loss, for a particular year. We then ask Jesus to heal it by "walking back in time." We forgive, and ask forgiveness if need be, then forget it. Gradually, the memories become less oppressive, and before long we feel free.

"Healing of memories" is unlike psychoanalysis in that, although it goes into the pain of the past, it goes beyond awareness to healing. It does not settle only for our being able to recognize the cause of our pain but, with believing and expectant faith, invites Jesus in to heal it.

7. Capitalize on all the dividends of positive memories.

It is not enough simply to eradicate the harm of negative memories. As neurological studies first conducted in the 1950s showed, the happy, fulfilling, hope-filled memories are also stored in our brains—and are probably more important because they are given less attention. As St. Ignatius explained, we should deliberately return to positive memories when we feel depressed and take in the love which is in those memories. This is what produces a change and opens us up to hope. We save only reminders of hope, happiness, and love, so boxes of old photos, family albums, dusty trophies, and other memorabilia are a good place to start the good memories. Take each picture and study it. Remember. Smile. Relive. Rejoice. Give God thanks for this personal gift. As a remembrance guide for the future—when the devil tries to convince you that nothing good has ever happened to you—you might want to write something of a cutline, giving the date, the people, the event, and any positive emotions associated with each photo or other item.

Prayer is both a gift of grace and a determined response on our part. It always presupposes effort. The great figures of prayer of the old covenant before Christ, as well as the mother of God, the saints and he himself, all teach us this: prayer is a battle.

Against whom? Against ourselves and against the wiles of the tempter who does all he can to turn man away from prayer, away from union with God.[1]

Catechism of the Catholic Church (#2725)

EIGHT

I Just Can't Pray Anymore

And when you pray, you must not be like the hypocrites; for they love to stand and pray in the synagogues and at the street corners, that they may be seen by men. Truly, I say to you, they have their reward. But when you pray, go into your room and shut the door and pray to your Father who is in secret; and your Father who sees in secret will reward you.

MATTHEW 6:5-6

This people honors me with their lips,
but their heart is far from me;
in vain do they worship me.

MATTHEW 15:8-9

Jack Templeton, ruddy and still quite athletic looking as he neared the age of sixty, was shocked to learn he had a rare malignancy of the blood that could prove fatal.

Almost overnight, it seemed, his personality changed from upbeat and even-tempered to that of an angry complainer.

Mostly, he felt betrayed by God. He had always been a faithful husband and had done a lot of volunteer work for the Church. He was doing his utmost to raise his children as good Christians.

"What did I do to deserve this?" he'd ask himself over and over. Worse than that, as he blurted out to the priest in confession, "I can't pray... not even if I force myself. If I died right now, I know I'd go straight to hell!"

Contrasting Jack's prayer dilemma is the story of an old illiterate peasant, crippled with arthritis, who would drag himself into a nearby chapel and just sit there for hours in silence. When asked what he did all that time, day after day, just facing the tabernacle, he'd reply, "I look at him. He looks at me. It makes us both happy."

Like a great many other believers, the man with the potentially fatal condition felt that salvation was something to be earned. He never knew what it was to have some kind of experiential relationship with Jesus. Therefore, he thought that since he could not concentrate on formal prayers and was unable to "pray right," his soul was doomed to condemnation. On the other hand, the serene old man, simply sitting in a pew, glowed with inward assurance that he communicated with God while not even whispering a word.

These two examples, quite obviously, are extreme glimpses of individual prayer life. Our personal prayer "portfolios" are as varied as our personalities, our environment, and the day-to-day challenges which all humans undergo. Nonetheless, we search for spiritual direction, go on retreats, and read books by spiritual masters in the hope of finding a way through some "desert" times or as a means of spiritual growth.

Many of us have come to realize, however, that it is in those very times when we don't feel like praying, or we simply cannot "find" the Lord, that there is the greatest potential for spiritual stretching down the line.

This is particularly true for those of us with an "apostolate of suffering." It applies to not only the disabled and chronically ill, but anyone thrust into sickness and rehabilitation whose normal spiritual orientation seems flattened by the steamroller events of life.

Setting Things Straight

In a nutshell, prayer is communicating with God personally. Even when done with others, it is a unique experience—which on one hand can be hurried, perfunctory, or sloppy, or deeply enriching on the other. "Praying is like talking to God on the phone," our younger son concluded at the age of five. "You gotta talk and listen. You hang up when you're done." (Hopefully, we are never done!)

More often than not, our problem is that we "pretend" at prayer, as Thomas Merton put it. There is a certain role-playing which can render it all very artificial, as Jesus well knew, when we honor God with our lips even when our hearts are far away.

In times of distress, extreme anxiety, or personal suffering it usually takes on another character. Our prayer is focused almost exclusively on ourselves, making our time at prayer more a session for physical, psychological, or even material evaluation. Instead of abandoning ourselves as we keep our eyes on the Lord, we find ourselves in an avalanche of thoughts that are really no prayer at all.

If we feel we have landed on spiritual quicksand (like Jack, the self-confident man who could not handle illness) we may think of God as a cop riding around in an unmarked car, ready to get us. If things are going well, we keep at a safe distance, thinking that if we ever find ourselves in a jam, there's always the "celestial 911" we can call.

"It sometimes happens that we treat God as though he were a fireman," Fr. Denis O'Brien, spiritual director of the American Life League, writes. "When we need him, we pull the alarm."[2]

Needless to say, while communication with God has different motivations and while it may take different forms and intensities, there is one basic component which makes it valid: It is an effort of a finite creature to contact an infinite, wise, powerful, and loving God.

It can be vocal, mental, meditative, or contemplative and it is ideally associated with Bible-reading. As Vatican II affirmed, "Prayer should accompany the reading of Sacred Scripture so that God and His beloved may talk together, for we speak to Him when we pray and He speaks to us when we hear the Word of God."[3]

Too many times we tackle prayer the way we program a VCR or load software. We assume that it is complicated, requiring in-depth study and incredibly precise actions to be successful. Small wonder then that we end up prattling some formal prayer to which we give no thought whatsoever—and gradually quit because we just "don't feel like it anymore."

Father O'Brien tells the story of a nun who was in the same convent as St. Jane Frances de Chantal. She decided to stay in her room rather than go to chapel for night prayers because she simply didn't feel like going.

"I haven't felt like praying for twenty-five years," St. Jane told her. "Now, my dear, let's go to the chapel."[4]

Feelings should not be forced, nor should any emotions which may or may not accompany our prayer. All that is expected is that we make every attempt to put God first and ourselves last, for as Scripture promises, he will not reject a humble and contrite heart (see Psalms 51:17). It is important to know that just because our prayer life does not please us at the moment, if it has been drastically changed because of illness or unavoidable circumstances which God allows, this does not mean that our prayer fails to please him.

Indeed, he may actually be drawing much closer just at a time when we consider him growing dim and remote. God is pleased with our sporadic, stumbling efforts. He is fully aware that we are trying to do the best we can!

In the spiritual classic, *The Way of Perfection*, St. Teresa of Avila writes, "For me prayer is an aspiration of the heart. It is a simple glance directed toward heaven, it is a cry of gratitude and love in the midst of trial as well as joy."[5]

In contemporary times, Peter Kreeft says of prayer, "The first rule for prayer, the most important first step, is not about how to do it, but just do it; not to perfect and complete it, but to begin it. Once a car is moving, it's easy to steer it in the right direction, but it's much harder to start it when it's stalled...."[6]

Looking to the Light

Throughout our lives we encounter plenty of spiritual potholes which jar us with worry and fear, and into which we sometimes sink, unable to pull out. As we grow in spiritual maturity, however, most people at least attempt to keep praying and not lose heart (as Jesus urges through his parable about the widow and the unjust judge in Luke 18). The deepest and ultimate pothole—one into which many in our modern world continually fall—is to accept the demonic notion that God doesn't really care about us. There are those tormenting thoughts like, "If God really loves me, why did he allow this marriage to end?" or "Why do other people get healed and not me?" or "After all I've suffered losing my job, you'd think God would give me a break."

Whenever there is a particularly difficult time in our lives, we seem to go through a progression of emotions which certainly has a bearing on how we pray. It can begin with fear and then move to anger when we are stripped of control and independence—and when others fail to meet our wants or expectations. This anger can easily be passed on to God, whom we inwardly envision as distant in our moment of great need.

It may be a long time before we are able to relinquish our expectations and to begin trusting in the expectations of a God whose constancy is not dependent on our feelings. Sooner or later there is no choice. We must come to the realization that God is the only answer to the problems and vicissitudes of life.

This is as true of our prayer lives as with everything else. It is he who stands patiently at the door of our hearts and knocks, waiting for us to let him in. The "doorknob" is on our side. If we welcome him into our hearts, Jesus does not stand in stiff propriety but warmly asks us to relax in his presence. His love and affirmation permeate our bruised and fickle hearts as he gently repeats the words of St. Augustine, "Our hearts are restless until they rest in thee."

Our Lord explains that all our inner restlessness has been allowed for a specific purpose, that of drawing us closer to himself by eliminating some illusions. He wants us to tear down any spiritual walls that we ourselves may have erected between us, any subtle spiritual props for which we take credit.

We may well have gone to prayer and invited God along on our terms rather than simply, humbly placing ourselves at his disposal. We may have gone well beyond approaching him with a grocery list of petitions, but it is also possible to have concentrated so much on preliminary prayer rituals that we all but forget the God for whom it is all being done!

For a long time I became adept at erecting such barriers. I

anticipated my morning quiet time and enthusiastically mastered physical relaxation techniques for use in meditation. It often lasted for hours (the phone off the hook) and left me in something of an altered state of consciousness. Severe leg spasms, as well as the arrival of our son and his family to share our home, made me put a reluctant end to this.

Only after Jesus allowed circumstances to intervene was I able to realize that my prayer was actually a prideful way of manipulating God. There are many people who benefit from some similar kind of Christian meditation or centering prayer. For me, I had to admit that it was not so much God himself who became my primary goal, but the hyper-relaxation or feeling I got.

How our wonderful Lord must smile at all our self-constructed prayer detours! Our "prayer pendulum" can swing from the far side of fear and distrust to the opposite position of self-satisfaction and spiritual pride. So he brings us back to himself, the true center, where we find ourselves humbly expressing prayers of adoration, contrition for our sins, thanksgiving for all his merciful love, and petitions for the specific needs of ourselves and others.

Day by day and year by year, God will perfect our prayer life, so long as we try to live every aspect of our lives in total abandonment to his will. St. Thérèse of Lisieux called this her "compass"—the only path leading to the "divine furnace" of God's love.

"It is the complete abandonment of a baby sleeping without fear in its father's arms," she wrote in her autobiography, *The Story of a Soul.* "Jesus does not demand great deeds. All he wants is self-surrender and gratitude."[7]

To surrender oneself totally to our loving God each day is not at all easy in the beginning. When we awaken we might say something like, "Thank you, Lord, for this new day. Help me to do your will." This prayer is good because it presumes a willingness to obey the laws of God and his Church and to accept the duties imposed by our particular state in life. It may take many years, however, before we can pray in earnest, "Lord, I hand over my life to you this day. May your perfect will be done in me, and in all that I think or do or say." (In every pain, problem, or perplexity.)

There is a radical difference between these two prayers. In the first, the concern is our doing God's will. The second is about God doing his will in us. He is the active one, we his instruments. This is not merely spiritual semantics, it is of utmost importance to those who have no choice but to suffer.

The attitude of surrender and abandonment can have almost medieval overtones unless we grasp the fact that, far from making us into inanimate robots of sorts, it unleashes incredible results in whatever the day brings. We may be the sick, the ignored, the powerless, and the misunderstood ones, but we possess God's power in speaking or acting or praying! Of such unimpressive souls, Jean-Pierre de Caussade writes, "The world thinks them useless and it seems as if they are. Yet it is quite certain that by various means and through hidden channels they pour out spiritual help on people who are often quite unaware of it and of whom they themselves never think. For those who have surrendered themselves completely to God, all they are and do has power. Their lives are sermons.... God gives a special force to all they say and do, even to their silence...."[8]

Such a total abandonment, however, is built on much hope and trust. "I am making myself dependent on your trust," Jesus told Sister Faustina when he appeared to her in Poland in the 1930s. "If your trust will be great, then my generosity will know no limitations."[9]

Anima Christi

Jesus, may all that is you flow into me.
May your body and blood be my food and drink.
May your passion and death be my strength and life.
Jesus, with you by my side, enough has been given.
May the shelter I seek be the shadow of your cross.
Let me not run from the love which you offer
But hold me safe from the forces of evil.
On each of my dyings shed your life and your love.
Keep calling me until the day comes when,
With your saints, I may praise you forever. Amen.

(traditional Catholic prayer)

Follow-up Action

1. Ask the Holy Spirit to "customize" your prayer time.

Like a pair of shoes, our prayer should fit us individually. While there are general guidelines for everyone—having regular prayer, reading Scripture, making use of the sacraments, etc.—we must never forget that the basic players in our prayer-drama are God and me. The important thing is our communication—even if only for a few quality minutes—and doing it the best way that it works for us. (Personally, I find a cup of coffee does wonders with any morning cobwebs in my brain!)

2. If possible, go beyond formal prayers.

God does not expect to hear only eloquent and grammatically perfect prayers from us. He prefers that we be ourselves and that we should pray simply, sincerely, and spontaneously. In fact, the more we can employ a conversational tone and speak to Jesus as we would to a very good friend, the more we will know him. And the more we know him, the more we love him.

Such were the convictions of Brother Lawrence, a barefoot seventeenth century kitchen helper in a Carmelite monastery, who said that anyone could build a "chapel" in the heart where they can develop the habit of conversing with God. In his famous classic *Practicing the Presence of God*, he details his experience of the "best friends" spirituality that permeated his life.

"The time of business is not different from the time of prayer," wrote Brother Lawrence. "In the noise and clatter of my kitchen, while several persons are at the same time calling for different things, I possess God in as great tranquillity as if I were upon my knees at the Blessed Sacrament."[10]

3. Try to make "the serenity prayer" a living prayer.

It may well be that we need to live out the basic things we profess in this prayer, which has been popularized through Alcoholics Anonymous:

> *Lord, grant me the serenity to accept the things I cannot change; the courage to change the things I can; and the wisdom to know the difference.*

We must learn to accept a past we cannot change, to live in the present and accept people as they are, and to use our pain victoriously. A radical change of mind brings a radical and truly courageous change of action through the Holy Spirit—who also gives us the wisdom to make sound, practical judgments.

4. Choose a personal "prayer project" and give it all you've got!

Though we may not see results on this earth, no prayer is ever wasted. Many think that the crumbling of Communist ideology was the effect of millions upon millions of rosaries asked by Our Lady of Fatima. Today, with an erosion of the value of life, we need a new prayer crusade!

Abortion, fetal experimentation, euthanasia, and other evils can only be stopped by prayer, often the prayer of many who appear useless, non-productive, and weak. United in purpose, however, we have the potential of being a formidable army of prayer warriors!

Instead of some collective goal to heal the evils in society, we may want to direct prayer for needy individuals as our project. This is what Joseph Hrdina, a cancer survivor now with an oncology support ministry in Newark's St. James Hospital, does. He certainly lives his own advice about being "extravagant" with healing prayers!

"Pray for everyone in the hospital or clinic you visit—staff and patients," he says. "Pray for your doctors and nurses. Pray and bless the chemotherapy you receive. Offer dozens of prayers for those who have lost the gift of prayer and for those who have no one to pray for them. Pray for the people who clean your room and the people who bring your meals. Pray for your relatives who are too chicken to visit you. Pray for those who hope you don't die at an inconveniently awkward time for them."[11]

5. When all prayer energy has fizzled out...

Great weariness, drugs, and a wide variety of medical procedures can induce a kind of heart-mind-spirit shriveling which makes conscious prayer all but impossible. So can sudden accidents.

I remember the time my knees buckled after stepping out of the shower and I fell backward, shattering the glass door. "Hon! Don't move!" my husband cautioned, and all I could manage was an "Oh God...!" as he carefully picked pieces of glass out of my back. Only some minutes later, when I could glimpse blood and glittering glass on the floor, did the prayer, "Jesus have mercy... Jesus have mercy..." repeat itself.

If we have formed the habit of quick ejaculations of words like "Praise you, Jesus" or the Jesus Prayer ("Lord Jesus Christ, Son of the living God, have mercy on me, a sinner"), it becomes second nature to repeat them when we are in serious trouble.

God hath ordered it that we may learn to
bear one another's burden; for no one is
without fault, no one but hath a burden;
no one is sufficient for himself.

Thomas à Kempis
Imitation of Christ

NINE

I Hate Being a Burden

Come to me, all you who labor and are heavy laden, and I will give you rest. Take my yoke upon you, and learn from me; for I am gentle and lowly in heart, and you will find rest for your souls. For my yoke is easy, and my burden is light.

MATTHEW 11:28-30

"**M**y friend was having a very tough time... two rebellious teens, their rebellion dipping into criminality. A job that didn't pay the bills to begin with was dissolving. His wife had severe health problems. Their parents—all four of them—were failing physically.

"Add to that the fact that my friend made his living in one of the helping professions. Every day, every hour, he was besieged with pleas for help.

"'I'm the one who needs help,' he said, 'I can't cope with this anymore. I lie awake at night dreading the next day. When I wake in the morning, I feel like pulling the covers over my head and disappearing. It's too much for me. I have nothing to give anymore.'"[1]

This very clear and seemingly insurmountable life situation is not unique in our society. It would appear that the percentage of people needing all kinds of help—especially teenagers and the elderly—is multiplying rapidly while family caregivers are extending themselves to the point of being overwhelmed. There are no longer normal hopes and dreams, only an inner anguish which all too often eradicates a consciousness of God. Left totally to one's resources alone, life seems like a hopeless blur.

"Connected with disappointment but moving to a different and deeper level, it can happen that when life becomes heavy and burdensome one loses the very will to believe," columnist Fr. Thomas McDonnell writes.[2]

True, while good Christians are hardly exempt from severe trials, we must never give the devil an edge by plummeting into despair, as though Jesus' victory on the cross were pointless. This becomes the cutting edge of our faith, for we *must* be a people of hope.

This is important in our modern world, where a fast-moving and inoperable social disease has infected even many medical professionals. It has been termed "cardiosclerosis" by Fr. McDonnell. The term means that the heart shrivels up with concern mostly for oneself, and at the same time grows with indifference to the suffering of others.

This "disease" is hardly new. Spiritual masters have long known about such a condition, one in which a person focuses on the self and the immediate rather than self-sacrifice for someone else. People are divided, therefore, between those who *must* be burdens and those who take willing and empathetic responsibility for them.

The suffering person needs hope-filled compassionate care, but let's face it, such virtues often prove somewhat scarce. It is not popular to shoulder "the cross of fidelity" for many of today's fragmented families. The end result is that this is absorbed by the person who is suffering, leaving irreparable feelings of guilt.

In such a climate, is it any wonder that life has become as disposable as plastic wrap?

Setting Things Straight

There is absolutely nobody on the face of this earth who is not (or has never been) a burden to someone else in some way. The infant screaming with an earache at three in the morning, the elderly mother who must be lifted onto the commode, the teenager tempted to commit suicide because absolutely nobody understands, the handicapped husband watching his wife wear herself out for the family, and so on.

Although we may not be aware of it, much of the desperation and hopelessness we all feel when everything seems too much comes from a worldly philosophy of life. We have absorbed a notion that difficulties or tragedies just shouldn't happen to us or those close to us. On some unconscious level we cling to the misconception that we are entitled to only the best. Paradise is seen as our right. And we think we should have it now!

No wonder we find ourselves exasperated and frustrated with the events of life. This applies both to those trapped in suffering as well as caregivers who feel trapped. Both cry out "Why? Why?" Neither has found personal strength to step beyond the pain, the anguish, and the apparent injustice. Neither has chosen to accept the status quo as part of God's plan.

"And yet, right in the midst of pain are the shafts of pure joy, the acts of generosity, of selflessness, and of heroism that reveal the face of Christ," Dr. Sheila Cassidy writes.

A former Maryknoll missionary, Dr. Cassidy endured political persecution and is now involved with hospice work. "From time to time, I am asked if my contact with so much suffering makes me doubt the existence of God... Paradoxically, this work has given me an ever deeper conviction of the existence of an all-powerful, all-loving God who has the whole world in his hands."[3]

This doctor does not deny that in order to come to such an appreciation of God, there is need for "costly loving" rather than counterfeit compassion which is now making swift inroads into the medical community. As medical care is presently developing, "costly loving" is not high on the scale of options. For example, would a doctor spend half an hour of his valuable time talking to a man who lives with an incurable disease when there are patients who will get well for sure and want to talk to him?

We may be among those marginal people who experience only medical "quick care," or others who have had a brush with counterfeit compassion. A friend recently told me of all the pressure (compassionately applied, of course) to have her baby aborted.

"Having your first child at thirty-eight is very risky, considering statistics," one doctor told her. "We can do some biogenetic tests, and if the fetus is defective... well, you wouldn't want your baby to live with a handicap, would you?" (At least three other nurses expressed the same concern, but eight-pound Paul was born absolutely perfect.)

With all the "medical-tech guns" there is a growing enthusiasm for eugenics—the perverse outcome of a kind of free-floating sentimentalization. Meanwhile, all of the elderly, the disabled, and the "hopeless" will, as euthanasia proponents hope, be quietly "eased away." We may not hear it articulated in this way on the evening news, but the tacit propaganda is that "the world would be much better off without them." (After all, the handicapped disturb the sense of the beautiful, and old people challenge the myth of perpetual youth!)

Looking to the Light

The life we have is in "earthen vessels," St. Paul said, making it clear that we can take no credit for its power. "We are afflicted in every way, but not crushed;... persecuted, but not forsaken;... struck down, but not destroyed;... always carrying in the body the death of Jesus, so that the life of Jesus may also be manifested in our bodies" (2 Cor 4:8-10).

In essence, there really is no way to experience the dying of Christ, with all that we must live through, without his supernatural grace. It is a grace, however, that is neither pre-packaged nor eternally complete. It can be received only with prayerful hope one moment at a time. After all, in the great prayer Jesus left us, the Lord's Prayer, he says we should ask the Father for only our *daily* bread. We thank him and then trust that when we pray the next day, he will supply the needs of tomorrow.

What if the same needs keep repeating themselves? Then we keep asking until things change and they no longer exist, or until new needs become apparent. Jesus assures us that we need not be afraid or ashamed of petitioning God over and over again.

For the badly hurting who are fully aware that they are a burden—be it physical or mental, be it temporary or terminal—one of the greatest needs is compassionate presence. This is not just the perfunctory kindness of a doctor "checking in" or a home health aide making lunch. Rather, it is a desperate need to be assured of being loved just as they are. They need

to see that their lives still have meaning and they need someone to help them discover the power to hope beyond circumstances, regardless of appearances.

A beautiful example came the time when a friend was at the
side of her husband's hospital bed. A priest had just left after
giving him the Sacrament of the Sick. It was their fifty-first
wedding anniversary and, holding his hand, Althea comment-
ed, "We never did celebrate our fiftieth anniversary, John....
Would you marry me all over again?" He smiled with, "I sure
would."

With that, she darted out the door and down the hall, coming back with a surprised chaplain who launched into, "Well, I
don't get many people wanting to repeat their vows after over
half a century... but sure, I can perform the ceremony. Right
here...?"

Their sincere repetition of "...in sickness and in health... till
death do us part" was extremely poignant and reassuring, not
only for this couple, but for their son and a nurse who stood in
as a witness. The priest left John's room singing.

"A person in pain needs someone to share the joyful
moments as well as times of hurting; someone neither senti-
mental nor overprotective; someone who is a sign of God's
tenderness and unending fidelity," says Jean Vanier, founder of
the famed L'Arche communities for mentally and physically
impaired adults.

There is no denying that a needy person presents a burden,
especially if the condition will not improve, at least in the fore-
seeable future. In the face of constant need, love and care
require family and friends to take a personal risk. It demands a
spirit of sacrificial love.

"We're afraid to love because in loving we commit ourselves
to another person, and that commitment means that something within us must die," as Vanier explains, "We give up

some of our comfort, our wealth, our time, our culture—perhaps our reputation or a measure of success, maybe even our friends."[4]

A neurologist friend said that this is particularly applicable in cases where one married partner has multiple sclerosis. In fact, he jarred my husband at a social gathering once when he asked, "Why did you stay in your marriage so long?"

"Because I love my wife," my husband responded.

"You are in a slim minority," the doctor explained. "Of all my married female patients with MS, not one husband has stayed. But of my male MS patients just about every one of their wives has remained committed."

This was not a controlled scientific survey, of course, but it may well show the natural nurturing instinct of wives. At any rate, this indicates true "costly loving"!

"There is no remedy more saving and effective to restoring hope and dignity to another than the healing touch of someone's compassionate presence in times of trouble," writes Sr. Jane Raphael Livingston. "It requires loving God above all things and our neighbor as ourselves, even when that love may be difficult."[5]

Prayer to the Paraclete

Holy Spirit, beloved Power of God, come!
You are my Helper, my Counselor, my Consoler, my Guide.
Quiet the fear and insecurity that pound on the door of
*   my heart.*
Strengthen me with your strength so that I will be able
*   to cope and endure.*
Enlighten my mind that I may see clearly all that you
*   require of me.*
Speak your words whenever I speak so that what I say may
*   be a source of joy and affirmation.*

*Instill in me a deeper faith, a truly living hope, and an
ever-growing desire for God.
Flood my heart with your love, so that all that I am,
all that I say, all that I do, will be a clear reflection
of Jesus. Amen.*

Follow-up Action

1. Reaffirm an inner determination to "choose life."

Regardless of the current status of "burdenhood" where we might envision ourselves, it is vital to keep repeating: "I will go on, according to God's purpose and plan." Like the repetition of advertising, it is almost auto-hypnotic and sticks in the brain. Psychologically, it is beneficial because it allows for control on the deepest level of our being. Spiritually, it opens the door for purer hope and trust in the God of the "impossible."

2. Act on the "life decision" to which you are committed.

When Jesus said we could not be his disciples unless we took up our own cross and followed him, he knew full well how many would just drag their cross, or drop it, or kick it angrily because it was not made of styrofoam or because it did not have little wheels on the bottom like some suitcases!

By prayerfully making our life decision and by cooperating in any practical therapy, we are doing what Jesus asks. Surprisingly, in the process we may actually be opening the way for his healing, because we do not stay stuck in a "shock gulley." For instance, while the dreaded prognosis of cancer will surely jar us, we hang on the fact that more than half of all Americans with a history of some kind of cancer have been cured. "If it's in God's perfect will, I'll be one of them," we tell ourselves.

We must think hope and speak hope to have hope. We enlist all possible assistance to our cause, including the saints and angels. For especially difficult or impossible cases, people have traditionally asked St. Jude for intercession. With the great prevalence of cancer in modern times, many others have discovered St. Peregrine, who was himself healed of bone cancer. Traditional prayer to St. Peregrine: "You were cured instantly of cancer by God's grace and unceasing prayer. In your gracious kindness, please ask the Lord to heal me also in body, mind, and soul."

3. Make a personal "burden review."

Many of us who are undergoing pain and difficulty of body and mind become captive to a "must" or "should" tyranny. We say things like, "You know I *must* have the window open two inches!" or "The therapist just left? She *should* remember that I can't reach that far for my crutches!"

In all probability our comments are valid, but if we sometimes put them on hold and ask the Spirit for enlightenment, we might see a different perspective. In retrospect, I came to realize that we burdeners often need not be overburdeners. For instance, my husband and sons, who were my caregivers during my worst periods of MS, were often irritated because I demanded something they were just about to do! Since then I've been enlisting my guardian angel to help with things like improvising instead of calling for a tray... or giving support when I try to stand.

After thinking through the practicalities of a given situation and being open to where we might be overburdening those who help us, we must at least make an effort to simplify or improvise things. When age weakened his grip, the noted artist Auguste Renoir painted with a brush strapped to his wrist!

4. Develop a listening/affirming ministry.

Those with illnesses or disabilities which are long-term but not life-threatening frequently find themselves used as the Lord's "healing helpers." This might be seen in a hospital clinic's waiting room, where a genial man in a wheelchair offers encouragement to a twelve-year-old who broke his leg playing hockey. Or a woman in for a post-mastectomy checkup listens empathetically to a young mother whose turban is a telltale sign of chemotherapy hair loss. Who better to give hope and encouragement? The need for some kind and non-judgmental person to listen to our problems is universal.

There is, likewise, a universal need to be affirmed in some way—certainly for the well, but much more the suffering. It is quite possible that our own need for affirmation may be lacking, and that is precisely why we can "feel" for the same need in others. And it is why God can use us in this area.

Scripture summarizes this with, "(God) comforts us in all our afflictions so that we may be able to comfort those who are in any affliction, with the comfort with which we ourselves are comforted by God" (2 Cor 1:4).

5. Utilize your unique gifts when growing old.

"The Masses you have attended throughout your life, the devout communions... the prayers... enable you to bestow right gifts,..." Pope John Paul II once told the elderly. "We need your experience and your insights. We need the faith which has sustained you and continues to be your light. We need your example of patient waiting and trust."[6]

While short-term memory diminishes somewhat with age, many seniors find they can remember things which happened as far back as childhood in vivid detail. These memories—personal events or historical stories—are very precious and should not be wasted. Instead of feeling obsolete and burdensome, therefore, we should all write down the special, joy-filled stories that come to mind. As they grow, grandchildren (and even great-grandchildren) are generally amazed and delighted—and have not only a new appreciation of history, but experience a tightening of family bonds.

Through all of this, my brothers and sisters, I am at peace and I can only account for that by looking upon it as a gift from God. People have asked me, "How can you explain this peace?" Three things come to mind.

First of all, you really have to trust the Lord. At an intellectual level we do. But at a much deeper, personal and emotional level, you have to learn to trust. If you don't have that trust, there's no way you can have that peace of mind.

The second thing is that, if you believe in the Lord and trust in the Lord, you should be able to see death as a friend, and not as an enemy. If the first is right and the second is right, the third follows: you have to let go. That letting go is not the easiest thing in the world.[1]

Cardinal Joseph Bernardin
October 23, 1996

What Do I Need to Do Before I Die?

Let not your hearts be troubled; believe in God, believe also in me. In my Father's house are many rooms; if it were not so, would I have told you that I go to prepare a place for you? And when I go and prepare a place for you, I will come again and will take you to myself, that where I am you may be also.

JOHN 14:1-3

Fear not, little flock, for it is your Father's good pleasure to give you the kingdom.

LUKE 12:32

It had been an incredibly long four years. There were eight operations and innumerable "procedures," some occurring during the winter of '96—which ended with a record snowfall that made driving hazardous. Althea would often just sleep at the hospital, on a cot next to John's bed, her whole life revolving around routines, nurses' schedules, test results, and prayer.

"As long as there's life, there's hope," Althea would insist each morning. "Now let's say our Rosary, John."

Doctors and the nursing staff hardly expected this seventy-five-year-old grandfather to survive so much bodily intrusion. The time finally came when nothing more could be done. Along with bags of health supplies and unfinished medications, he was sent home to die.

"We'll just keep praying," Althea would say each day, as a parade of visiting nurses, therapists, and homemaker aides came to the door. For a couple of weeks, John seemed to be responding, eating well, and sitting up.

Then came the morning which capped a pain-wracked night when neither one could sleep. "Come close, Althea," he said with calm assurance, stroking her cheek, "I love you... the time has come... it's his will."

"Do you want me to call the children?"

He nodded, and soon the room was filled with grown sons and a daughter, standing around the bed as he lay without speaking. It was the next day, however, when Althea sat alone with the only man she had ever loved and prayed the Way of the Cross that John was taken Home.

"It was such a beautiful death," she said later. "He was ready... he was totally at peace. He had such a wonderful look on his face."

This is precisely how the death of a Christian should be. Unfortunately, for many people today, "The hereafter has become a joke," as one commentator put it, "reducing it to something of a nervous uncertainty at wakes of good friends."

This was not so for most of the two millennia of Christianity. The notion of some kind of eternal life was not only envisaged, it was the core expectation on which religion and morality were based.

Modern society, on the other hand, thinks mostly in terms of the finite, where everything is bound by limitation—be it a personal computer or a "meaningful relationship." Obsolescence is planned and eternity is non-existent, especially for the X-generation.

If we concentrate exclusively on the present time and this known world, we may call ourselves "Christian," but we are really "secular." We forget the destiny and purpose for which we have been created. And we are part of what has been termed "the most widespread and the most insidious heresy of our modern age."

"Even those of us who in theory are struggling against secularism are often its accomplices or victims," writes Fr. Raniero Cantalmessa. "We have been 'worldlified'; we have lost the sense of a taste for, familiarity with, eternity."[2]

There should come a time, however, when we are no longer satisfied with a superficial belief system. In our struggle in life, we need to enter "deep waters," to ask ourselves some gut-honest questions:

Do we really believe what the Church teaches about life after death?

Can we actually count on some physical resurrection in an eternal dimension?

Will our body and soul be joined in the same glorified way as Jesus' was?

Is it superstition or wishful thinking to believe the "me" I now know will go on forever, as the Bible promises?

Can I do something to prepare for and enhance my eternity right now?

If these questions seem preposterous and too esoteric for "regular" Christians, then it clearly indicates how far we have gone in exchanging true reality for that which is as fake as tinsel. Whether we realize it or not, what we believe about eternity affects our living now. It has a very profound effect on the way we deal with pain, with loss, or with anything that requires commitment and personal courage.

Setting Things Straight

"We have lost the measure of eternity, and so earthly things and suffering easily depress our spirit," Fr. Cantalamessa says. "Everything strikes us as being too heavy and excessive."[3]

We are living in a time of choose-it-yourself ethics. But to consider one's beliefs about life and death as inviolable is foolish. Let's face it, there is just too much pressure—both overt and subtle—to conform to the majority opinion. It would seem that to be politically correct we all must now get on the new moral order bandwagon, agreeing that human authority over life and death is absolute. God's unquestioned sovereignty—traditionally held through all of Judeo-Christian history—becomes subordinate at best. At worst, his authority is simply dismissed as irrelevant.

As followers of Christ, we must not be blinded by buzz words. Our right is to be alive until our natural end, not to choose the time and manner in which we die! We are merely stewards of the life which God has entrusted to us, not its terminators! But because we are immersed in a world that is devaluing life as never before, we must examine life issues long before we are in a position to make concrete decisions for ourselves or others.

For years now the media has been saturated with stories

about terminally ill people whose "loving" family members "bravely" defied the law and acceded to their wishes for assisted suicide. They had doctors pull the plug on life-support machines or had feeding tubes removed so they would quite literally starve to death. Handicapped infants have been left unfed and uncared for until they died.

Basically, the moral door that was propped open by egalized abortion has opened wide. We are entering a new millennium, in which "killing" and "curing" are gradually becoming interchangeable. Our laws and court decisions are fast reflecting this ominous trend.

"To destroy the boundary between healing and killing would mark a radical departure from longstanding legal and medical traditions of our country, posing a threat of unforeseeable magnitude to vulnerable members of our society," the Catholic bishops warned in 1991.[4]

Concurring with them was a group of Christian and Jewish theologians, philosophers, and legal scholars who made a clear distinction between killing and allowing to die. "In relating to the sick, the suffering, the incompetent, the disabled, and the dying, we must relearn the wisdom that teaches us always to care, never to kill," they exhorted in their Declaration on Euthanasia. "Although it may sometimes appear to be an act of compassion, killing is never caring," they concluded.[5]

Both individuals and families will inevitably be affected by death "choices." For economic reasons if no other, euthanasia "will shortly become the way American society rids itself of 'burdensome lives' at the other extremity of life," Dr. Joseph Stanton, M.D. declared.[6]

Whether "assisted" or otherwise, suicide is the most unnatural death choice—be it an ailing and depressed widower or a confused adolescent. To both, life seems pointless and perhaps filled with cruelty and lovelessness. The elderly man considers himself nothing but a selfish coward, especially after his son's comment, "I see the patient next door had the respirator shut off. Guess he doesn't want to bankrupt his kids."

As for the adolescent, things such as peer pressure along with a high school death and dying class can push him over the edge. This may well be what happened to the son of an acquaintance, who blurted out one day, "Mom, what would you do if I said I was going to kill myself?" Because he seemed so sensible, she laughingly replied, "I'd kiss you good-bye!" That night he took out his father's hunting gun and shot himself.

It is a sad fact that most suicide victims had temporary and treatable cases of depression or other psychological problems. According to the American Association of Suicidology, for some 93 percent of all people who commit suicide, it is not a rational choice but a desperate plea for affirmation and under-standing.[7]

This shows an incredible failure of civilized society—especially when we hear of death purveyors like Dr. Jack Kevorkian. Two of the women whom he "assisted" early on had MS, but their symptoms seemed neither permanent nor unbearable—their suicides were more like anguished pleas for love and understanding. Instead of help and hope, they were given the false refuge of death.

In the classic film, *It's a Wonderful Life*, George Bailey, who is on the brink of suicide, has an angelic revelation. He is shown the secret heroism of his sustained commitment to life, and how people in his town would be enormously deprived if he were not there. This clearly exemplifies St. Thomas Aquinas' conclusion that self-destruction is wrong, not only because it is contrary to human nature, but because it deprives the rest of society of that person's unique existence.

But what of those people—both young and old—who are

in a coma or seem trapped in that in-between world, a "persistent vegetative state"? We cannot deny that there are many heart-wrenching cases; many agree with the medical technician who told me, during an electroencephalogram he was completing on me, "When a portion of the brain is not responding, the patient is better off dead."

This may be a common belief, but it fails to take into account other important factors. A recent survey reported in the *Archives of Neurology* indicated that 58 percent of the PVS (persistent vegetative state) subjects had regained consciousness after anywhere from a couple of months to three years.[8] Even if they had not, how-ever, there is no empirical evidence to show what a patient was actually experiencing during the time of apparent unawareness.

Things are not as they often appear. This was personally verified after I had a second-trimester miscarriage, when emergency room doctors were about to give up trying to transfuse blood because my veins were collapsed. How desperately I wished I could have at least fluttered an eyelash, anything to let them know I was still alive, as I shouted in my mind, "Don't give up! I'm here!"

Tied in with comas and PVS conditions is the understanding and interpretation of exactly what constitutes death. Before modern medical advances, the traditional standard for the determination of death was a permanent end to respiration and heartbeat. It proved that the whole brain was no longer functioning.

Today many people are declared "brain dead" even when the brain stem, which regulates blood pressure, temperature, endocrine, thyroid, and adrenal activity, is still functioning normally. It is this group that appears most vulnerable in the current impetus for euthanasia.

How important is it for those of us who are impaired to be

aware of all this? Every bit as important as being informed that the woman in the apartment beneath ours has just discovered termites!

Unlike termites, however, our eventual death cannot be "exterminated." It is a part of the human condition, but as Dr. Joanne Lynn described in the *New England Journal of Medicine,* "I am impressed by how well people can live while dying." (She participated in the care of some two thousand terminal patients, nearly all in hospice or home care settings.)[9] Happily hospice can remove paralyzing fears when we arrive at that final chapter of this journey of life.

"Those who would have us believe that death is necessarily accompanied by unbearable pain and suffering and that euthanasia or assisted suicide are the only compassionate alternatives are just plain wrong!" according to Dr. E. Joanne Angelo, a psychiatric consultant for Boston's Good Samaritan Hospice for well over ten years. "I have seen how the compassionate care by the hospice staff has enabled patients to live out their lives with serenity and peace, surrounded by those they love until natural death occurs."[10]

Looking to the Light

There are three special passages of the Bible that can be "life givers" of the Spirit to those of us who are in some extreme condition. It would be well to so interiorize them that they become literal life insurance when the monumental distractions of incapacitation are sure to come somewhere down the road:

1. None of us lives to himself, and none of us dies to himself.... whether we live or whether we die, we are the Lord's (Rom 14: 7).

2. "I am the resurrection and the life; he who believes in me, though he die, yet he shall live" (Jn 11: 25, 26).

3. Death is swallowed up in victory....O death, where is thy sting? (1 Cor 15:54-55)

Jesus has singlehandedly conquered the devil's most potent weapon against humanity—the fear of death—by his death and resurrection. All the hoping and trusting which he has been perfecting within us, therefore, are weapons to defeat panic when the time comes. If nothing else, we can hold on to these two absolute truths: we belong to God, and our lives are to be changed but not ended.

These are not merely pious platitudes. They are our lifeline to cling to when we are about to enter the "process of dying." Like being born, dying is an experience which we must, ultimately, go through alone. Nobody can take the place of an infant whose warm and self-sufficient abode must be exchanged for the sensual world of sounds, lights, and dependency. Likewise, no person or machine can stop or take our place in the inevitable transition we all must make from life to eternity.

The timing for this "great transition" is God's prerogative alone. He who has numbered our days before the first had even begun in this world knows when our souls are ready. He who is the great Producer/Director/Playwright of life has planned our time on the stage of earthly life with infinite love and care. He yearns for us to trust him, especially with the "last scene, last act" of our appointed time.

Humanly speaking we would like to run the show. We would, almost assuredly, write a script for ourselves with a long, enjoyable, successful, and healthy life—and with death coming painlessly, quietly, in our sleep. We would never conceive a tragedy, like that of a grieving father having a heart attack over the grave of a ten-year-old son who drowned while swimming.

There is no doubt that such horrendous stories do litter life. Yet, in the perspective of our loving Lord, many were needed so there could be eternal triumphs. Every "why" is answered. If we were writing the script, however, how could we know about the secret spiritual interaction which may be occurring near death? Anything dealing with accelerated spiritual awareness at such a time is considered merely a person's personal religious life. It is generally dismissed by doctors and even some theologians who take their opinions rather uncritically.

"There may be no cognitive action we can detect, but that does not mean a person's soul is not interacting with God," a retired doctor friend once told me. "This is a sacred time zone in my estimation, and it should not be cut short for the sake of cost-containment, nor even for donating of organs."

As this world considers it, dying can be much too long and messy—like birth—yet we see an awareness of the infinite and sacred in both. However subliminal, God's power is present.

For the person involved, a "bridge of time" appears necessary to move from this world to the other radically different one. St. Paul describes our eternal home, "What no eye has seen, nor ear heard, nor the heart of man conceived, what God has prepared for those who love him" (1 Cor 2:9).

He also writes about what will happen when we exchange our citizenship on earth for that of Heaven, "Now we see dimly in a mirror, but then face to face. Now I know in part; then I shall understand fully even as I have been fully understood" (1 Cor 13:12) and "[He] will bring to light the things now hidden in darkness and will disclose the intentions of the heart. Then every man will receive his commendation from God" (1 Cor 4:5).

To accept God's one-way ticket and to claim these beautiful promises, we need enough time to pack spiritually, according to Lillibeth Navarro, a disability rights activist. She ends a description of her grandfather's truly dignified death by saying, "I shudder to think of what delicate processes, unseen by the naked eye, we disrupt and preempt when we, in our haste, as mere human beings, rush to terminate life's natural processes."[11]

These "natural processes" are carefully guarded by the many hospices in this country. "The body may be unconscious, but one's soul is clear as a bell," as Rev. Paul von Lobkowitz, a Colorado hospice director, puts it. "After 30 years of working in hospice, the thing that still amazes me is at the moment of death, there is a presence in the room, a lightness when the soul leaves the body."[12]

This would appear to confirm the many after-life experiences (NDE or near-death experiences) which have been written about in recent years. Some doctors say this is merely erratic brain activity which cannot be verified. But this does not explain why those who were agnostics and atheists lead radically transformed lives when they return. We do not know the answers. We should not base our faith on these accounts, but on biblical and Church teaching.

Hope Fulfilled

Your ways are not our ways, and your thoughts are definitely not our thoughts.

They are immensely better and purer and higher.

How could it be otherwise for the one who holds the stars in the palm of his hand?

As I scan my "life map" and embark on this, my last winding path, I am no longer afraid. I do not feel alone.

Jesus, your loving presence fills me to overflowing. What joy you bring!

It is the last lap of my journey into eternity!

My going may be slow, soul-wrenching. Or with sudden shock, an instant untimely end. It can come to cap endless years of tears,

And it may be a welcomed yet fearful final curtain.

Or death may invite me gently, softly, as in a dream.

You know, dear God, it has all been decided. You planned my coming home from the moment I became a miraculous speck of life.

For this I praise you, my God. I thank you.

I hope in you alone, my refuge and my consolation.

Suddenly, Jesus, your loving arms embrace me and all is light, with a beauty beyond telling and music not meant for earthly ears.

A fire of love consumes me. I am saturated with your living waters.

At last, at last, you help me to see with your vision, Lord.

You show me the "why" of so many things that once concerned me and gave so much pain. These too were gifts!

Soon my spirit floats in indescribable bliss! I am in the "eternal now"!

I am safely Home!

Follow-up Action

1. Accept in your deepest self that earthly life must end sometime, somehow, somewhere.

This is neither fatalistic nor morbid, so long as it involves a mature understanding and a healthy acceptance. We can get a wide variety of healings all through life, but there comes a time for the perfect healing—our last healing—in the life to come. Only in Heaven will every tear be wiped away. And this will not come in some kind of New Age haze, nor through reincarnation—it will come only through Jesus Christ, our Lord, who has shown us the way.

2. Determine to cherish each new day and count it a gift!

"Oh God, the sun is shining today!" Carol exclaimed when her bedroom shade was lifted. "Today your gift is like a shiny new penny!" These were the words of a dear friend who, after surviving uterine cancer for ten years—was now told she had about four days to live. This was the fifth day. God had other plans, for although she could no longer eat or have normal bodily functions, she lived five more months and was miraculously lucid to the end. In the interim she was the catalyst in healing flawed family relationships and even religious bigotry, singing praise songs only a matter of hours before she died.

Bishop Stanley Ott of Baton Rouge, who also struggled with terminal cancer, said, "I have come to savor a little more of each day, of each moment—every sunshine, every ceremony, every person I come into contact with. I can't begin to express my thanks to God for letting me serve him all these years in health, and now in sickness, I shall continue, as long as I am able."[13]

3. While you still can, take care of all "unfinished business."

"The desire to end one's life well, to make something finished, or... to hand one's life over to God... I think can be very significant, even beautiful," theologian John Carmody said. He wrote the book *Conversations with a Dying Friend* shortly before learning that he himself had a terminal illness.[14]

As many a priest or counselor will attest, terminal patients often have painful regrets about leaving something undone. Sometimes it concerns worldly affairs, but usually it revolves about the spiritual realm. Since this can hamper God's grace at a time when it is most needed, the first assignment should be a complete spiritual housecleaning.

Any animosities, festering resentments, or unforgiveness must go. Unsaid apologies have to be voiced in a direct and forthright way. Positive thoughts and expressions of love—usually to those who are closest—ought to be put into words. There is no longer time to hide behind "Well, that's how I am" and continue the usual black humor or sarcasm which shielded honest feelings all your life. You can still change with God's help. Try to understand that a few kind and tender words of love can be the most valuable legacy one can leave. It can eradicate many years of insensitivity and psychological neglect.

4. Make full use of the church's sacraments towards the end.

Sometimes it is very reassuring to have a priest hear your general confession, something of a "lifetime review" in which contrition is again voiced about the most significant and troublesome sins. This is not an absolute necessity, since with each confession that is made God forgives one's sins and throws them "as far as the east is from the west." However, it may be spiritually enriching and psychologically beneficial to hear an absolution after one reiterates sincere contrition for a lifetime of choosing self over God.

The Sacrament of the Sick is especially important now as Viaticum, the Eucharistic "food for the journey," is given. It allows complete confidence, furthermore, that whatever temporal punishment (in purgatory) still due to sin is removed.

This is truly a "happy death," when life's ledger is perfectly balanced, when we are divested of all earthly investments and rid ourselves of any cumbersome or unnecessary spiritual baggage. We can now be prepared and fully anticipate citizenship in Heaven!

5. Understand and accept what the Church officially teaches about death, medical intervention, and euthanasia.

Teaching that Applies to All

- There is a stewardship responsibility we owe to God for the gift of life.
- Competent adult patients have the primary right and responsibility about their health care decisions.
- In conscience we are required to use appropriate and ordinary means to prolong and care for life when there is reasonable hope of benefit. This is not excessively burdensome (food, water, bed rest, pain medication, hygiene, etc.).
- There is no obligation in conscience to undergo or continue extraordinary means to prolong and care for life. This includes treatment which is excessively burdensome (treatment involving severe pain, risk, severely disabling effects, etc.), and offers little hope of any benefit.
- Church teaching defines euthanasia as "an action or an omission which of itself or by intention causes death in order that all suffering may in this way be eliminated." An "action" could be a lethal injection or overmedication. An "omission" can be deliberately withholding antibiotics (as in severe pneumonia) with the intention of causing death in an otherwise non-dying patient.

Teaching that Applies to Individual Cases

It is important to realize that many medical procedures now considered *ordinary* may still be considered *extraordinary* from an ethical point of view. For example, dialysis was once experimental but is now quite common. Likewise, it is easy today to provide food and water by inserting feeding tubes. If there is clear evidence, however, that feeding and hydration are ineffective and have no value to the patient, stomach tubes need not be inserted. This could happen if a person's body simply cannot assimilate either liquids or nourishment, or if the shutting down of vital signs has begun and death is imminent.[15]

Advance Delegation for Health Care

It is both wise and charitable to delegate someone who knows well our views on life and death (in accordance with Church teaching) to act as a health care proxy in the event that we can no longer make our own treatment decisions. *Do not use a living will because it can be greatly misinterpreted.* In effect, a reasonably healthy person who signs a living will makes a death decision when it is impossible to know what the future medical situation may be! Instead, a Durable Power of Attorney document or authorization for an Advance Directives for Health Care Decisions is preferable. Copies of these, along with clear explanations of Catholic teaching on the issue may be procured from the Pope John Center for the Study of Ethics in Health Care as well as the Value of Life Committee. The important thing to remember is that an advance directive should neither endorse—nor even open the door to possible endorsement of—euthanasia.[16] (See details in notes.)

Final Follow-up Action

1. Find inner peace on a new spiritual plateau.

When practical affairs are in order and all spiritual loose ends have been tied up and resolved, we may be ready for what Fr. Thomas McDonnell calls the "spirituality of substitution." This is the vocation lived by many shut-ins who take their place as "substitutes" for all the indifference and rejection of God by so many other people. They join their frustration to the frustration and pain of Jesus for the sake of the Church. As Jesus said to St. Catherine of Siena, "It is by means of my servants... that I would be merciful to the world and reform my bride the Church."[17]

Our spiritual life now becomes incredibly simple and most profound. With hearts totally given to Jesus, we become valuable instruments of peace and clear channels of his healing love.

A vivid example was a blind woman I knew who, though in her nineties, kept a police scanner on the headboard of her bed. She prayed for every "poor laddy" in trouble. When she herself was ready to die—and she knew it—she asked the Lord, "Hold it for another week, dear Jesus. Jamie's gettin' married on Saturday. If you take me now, it'll spoil the weddin'." She died in her sleep on Sunday night after the wedding.

This old woman truly had a ministry of love. Like her, many of those waiting to go home to the Lord can direct his healing to those most wounded or needy with nothing more than a quiet prayerful thought. Indeed, since God is the "reader of hearts," one's spiritual life can expand to immense heights through just such utter simplicity and childlike trust. And is this not what he asks to enter his Kingdom?

2. Be willing to let go of life in a loving and purposeful way.

It has been said that the only things you can hold in your dead hands are the things you have given away. This is how we can store up treasures in Heaven! In certain cases, however, there seem to be legitimate reasons for not being willing to give away some treasure. In fact, it would appear absolutely impossible unless we first "negotiate" with God. Like the young husband and father who has little chance of surviving some new surgical technique, but who will surely die without it. He "bargains" with God and is graced with accepting "whatever happens" only by accepting the fact that, in his perfect plan, God will provide for his family.

Many others must give away being aware of each diminishment. We may have been given a "mean survival time" of months or years, yet there is a sense of complete helplessness as little by little our former self erodes. So, do we seethe in anger at the approaching end, or simply acknowledge what is happening and relinquish it to God?

One of the hardest things to lose is one's ability to think clearly most of the time. Needed pain medications can play a big part, of course, but there may be those stretches of time when we know that we can't think right.

A friend's mother, a brilliant translator most of her adult life, went from depression to rage when it dawned on her what was happening to her mind. "I brought her tape recorder to the hospital," my friend said, "and when I played tapes of sacred music she became completely calm and serene."

Another woman with Alzheimer's would suddenly focus on her husband and pay attention whenever he would read from her well-worn Bible. Several times she smiled and nodded as if in agreement when he read something which she had underlined years ago.

3. Allow yourself to anticipate what is coming.

If and when you can think clearly enough, deliberately immerse your thoughts in Heaven; in Jesus, your tremendous Lover; in the Blessed Mother whom you will see as clearly as anyone on earth; in meeting your favorite saints who have interceded for you; in loved ones who died and are waiting; and in your guardian angel, whose help and patience you will finally appreciate. This is not foolish escapism. It is like naturally anticipating an eternal vacation, one the angels have always hoped for you!

> *Our Father, protect us all the day long*
> *till the shades lengthen and evening comes*
> *and the fever of life is over*
> *and our work is done.*
> *Then by your mercy grant us*
> *a safe lodging, a holy rest*
> *and peace at last.*

Cardinal Newman

Hippocrates Rises Anew: "The Still Relevant Hippocratic Oath"

by Joseph R. Stanton, M.D.,
E. Joanne Angelo, M.D.,
Marianne Luthin, M. Ed.

Revered as the Father of Medicine, Hippocrates (460-377 B.C.) is without question the most famous physician in antiquity. Regardless of the specific authorship of the famous Oath, that it comes down to us from that era is denied by none. Undeniable also is the fact that it profoundly influenced the practice of medicine across recorded history.

"Throughout the primitive world, the doctor and the sorcerer tended to be the same person. He with the power to kill had power to cure, including specially the undoing of his own killing activities," according to anthropologist Margaret Mead.

She calls the Oath, however, "a priceless possession of society which we cannot afford to tarnish, but society is always attempting to make the physician into a killer—to kill the defective child at birth, to leave sleeping pills beside the bed of the cancer patient.... It is the duty of society to protect the physician from such requests."

So it can be seen that the appearance of the Oath (c. 400 B.C.) represented a clear dividing line after which medicine was unalterably committed to protecting life and never deliberately killing—in simple grandeur: *I will give no one a deadly medicine even if asked, nor counsel any such thing; I will not give a woman a pessary to induce abortion...*"

The oath became the gold standard of moral and ethical behavior to which all physicians who took it were bound. Where lived up to, it protected patient, family, physicians, and society. Where violated, as it was massively this century in the Third Reich, the darkest chapters were written in medical history, culminating in physicians in the dock charged and found guilty of "crimes against humanity."

Medicine reacted vigorously. At Geneva in 1949, the unchanging principles of the Oath were restated in the unanimously adopted *Medical Declaration of Geneva* with its additional magnificent line "I will maintain the utmost respect for human life from the time of its conception..."

During the current century the Oath was explained away and essentially dismissed. The U.S. Supreme Court proclaimed that no one knew (or by implication could know) when an individual human life began and constructed a decision as if what lives and grows in the human womb in human pregnancy could not possibly be human, alive, and genetically unique. Thus did abortion become America's most commonly performed surgical procedure (1.5 million per year) and the philosophy of Roe v. Wade its most lethal export. The Court's decision effectively overturned laws existing in all fifty states, reversing legal protection of the child *en ventre sa mere* in American law.

Why did medicine not reject the court's assault on its

precious ethical heritage? Medicine had not been immune to the great social forces then at work. Radical feminism, large-scale distortion of "rights" with a downplaying of personal responsibility had all become dominant features of the society.

Fewer and fewer medical schools administered the Oath to its graduates. After all, how could one vow fidelity to an Oath rejecting that which was now upheld as a constitutional right and an expression of individual freedom? So the abortion age (and the growing trend in favor of euthanasia which it spawned) swept across Western civilization.

Then slowly at first, but with ever increasing power, a perception developed that something was wrong. A demand for the restoration of "moral values" ensued—even in countries like Russia. With the implosion of communism came "the restoration of the priority of universal moral principles" in the now-mandated "Promise of Russian Physicians." Another example was the British Medical Association where the physician head of Ethics has called for restoration of the ancient Oath.

Meanwhile in the United States, at least twenty-five "substitute oaths" have been published. None were judged to claim true fidelity to the time-honored Oath and all failed the test of wide-spread acceptance. One, for example, proclaimed the oxymoron, "I shall always have the highest respect for human life and remember that it is wrong to terminate life in certain circumstances, permissible in some and an act of charity in others."

Finally, the Value of Life Committee sought the opinions of a great many scholars and physicians, including distinguished authors of medical/ethical articles and texts. And the "A.D. 1995 Restatement of the Oath of Hippocrates" was born.

Providing a unique opportunity for dialogue—especially with medical school students—this copyrighted Oath has been requested by thousands of physicians throughout English and Spanish speaking countries. It was a most felicitous coincidence, moreover, that it came out simultaneously as it did with Pope John Paul's *Evangelium Vitae.*

In this encyclical the Pope summons health care personnel "to be guardians and servants of Life," referring to *"the still relevant Hippocratic Oath" which requires every doctor to commit himself (herself) to absolute respect for human life and its sacredness"* (par. 89).

So it is that the spirit of Hippocratic, ethical medical practice may be undergoing a second spring after a long winter of malaise. Let us pray that this is so and that what has been a labor of love may bear it full fruit across the next millennium.

Excerpted from a paper presented by representatives of the Value of Life Committee, Boston, at the Third World Congress of Pro-Life Movements, Rome, October 2-4, 1995. Joseph R. Stanton, M.D. was an associate clinical professor of medicine at Tufts Medical School and is a member of the board of National Doctors for Life. E. Joanne Angelo, M.D., a psychiatrist with a Boston practice, is on the faculty at Tufts medical school and the staff of St. Elizabeth's Hospital, Boston. Marianne Luthin, M.Ed., is an officer of Women Affirming Life and president of the Value of Life Committee.

A.D. 1995 Restatement of the Oath of Hippocrates

I SWEAR in the presence of the Almighty and before my family, my teachers and my peers that according to my ability and judgment I will keep this oath and stipulation.

I RECKON all who have taught me this art equally dear to me as my parents and in the same spirit and dedication to impart a knowledge of the art of medicine to others. I will continue with diligence to keep abreast of advances in medicine. I will treat without exception all who seek my ministrations, so long as the treatment of others is not compromised thereby, and I will seek the counsel of particularly skilled physicians where indicated for the benefit of my patient.

I WILL FOLLOW that method of treatment which according to my ability and judgment I consider for the benefit of my patient and abstain from whatever is harmful or mischievous. I will neither prescribe nor administer a lethal dose of medicine to any patient even if asked nor counsel any such thing nor perform act or omission with direct intent deliberately to end a human life. I will maintain the utmost respect for every human life from fertilization to natural death and reject abortion that deliberately takes a unique human life.

WITH PURITY, HOLINESS, AND BENEFICENCE I will pass my life and practice my art. Except for the prudent correction of an imminent danger, I will neither treat any patient nor carry out any research on any human being without the valid informed consent of the subject or the appropriate legal protector thereof, understanding that research must have as its purpose the furtherance of the health of that individual. Into whatever patient setting I enter, I will go for the benefit of the sick and will abstain from every voluntary act of mischief or corruption and further from the seduction of any patient.

WHATEVER IN CONNECTION with my professional practice or not in connection with it I may see or hear in the lives of my patients which ought not be spoken abroad I will not divulge, reckoning that all such should be kept secret.

WHILE I CONTINUE to keep this Oath unviolated may it be granted to me to enjoy life and the practice of medicine with the blessings of the Almighty and respected by my peers and society, but should I trespass and violate this Oath, may the reverse be my lot.

Copyright Value of Life Committee Inc.
760 Highland Ave., Needham, MA 02194.
Phone: (617) 444-3348

NOTES

TWO

1. *The Annals of Internal Medicine,* January 31, 1995, cited by Kathleen Howley in "No Arguing with Computer in Right to Die Cases," *The Pilot,* Boston: Living Word Syndicate, March 5, 1995, 15.
2. "The Ancient Company of Physicians," *The Catholic World Report,* April 1995, 49.
3. "The Ancient Company of Physicians," 50.
4. Leo Alexander, M.D., in Medical Foreword *To Touch the Hem of His Garment,* Mary Drahos (Mahwah, N.J.: Paulist 1983), 7.

THREE

1. Francois Mauriac, re: Holy Thursday, *An Intimate Remembrance* (Manchester, N.H.: Sophia Institute Press, 1992).
2. C.S. Lewis, cited by Francis Martin, "The Mystery of Suffering," *New Covenant,* April 1992.
3. Merlin Carothers, *Power in Praise* (Escondido, Calif.: Merlin R. Carothers, 1972), 70.
4. St. John of the Cross, *Dark Night of the Soul,* 2.7.3.
5. Woodene Koenig-Bricker, "God Gave Me the Strength I Needed," *Our Sunday Visitor,* September 13, 1992.

F O U R

1. Raphael Simon, O.C.S.O., M.D. *Hammer and Fire (Toward Divine Happiness and Mental Health)* (New York: P.J. Kennedy & Sons), 202-203.
2. For Catholic psychiatric help, Divine Mercy Treatment Centers, Steubenville, OH, 43952 Phone, 1-800-MERCY-4-U; also, Assn. of Christian Therapists, 3700 East Ave., Rochester, N.Y., 14618, Phone (716) 381-8590.

F I V E

1. William F. Hogan, C.S.C., "Woman of Compassion," *Spiritual Life,* Vol. 42, #4, Winter 1996, Discalced Carmelite Friars, Inc., Washington, D.C.
2. Fr. Joseph Hayden, S.J., as quoted by Lou Jacquet, "Finding Growth through Chronic Pain," *Our Sunday Visitor,* January 24, 1993.

S I X

1. Jane E. Brody, "Putting the emphasis on assisted living with M.S.," *New York Times,* October 23, 1996, C11.
2. Jessica Shaver, "Couldn't Kill," *The Family,* January 1992, 12. To contact Giana Jesson for tapes or concert schedule: Alive! Ministries, P.O. Box 4264, San Clemente, CA 92672, phone (714) 847-8835.
3. Dr. Joseph Stanton, "The New Untermenschen," *Human Life Review,* Fall 1985.
4. Patricia Trece, *Even Disabled, the Christian Is Never Useless* (Pecos, N.M.: Dove, 1990).

5. Mother Teresa's "Sick and Suffering Co-Workers," US contact: Agnes Hynes, 9111 S. Harding Ave., Evergreen Pk., IL 60642, Phone: (708) 636-9111. Also for Vocations for women with disabilities: Sisters of Jesus Crucified, Regina Mundi Priory, Devon, PA and St. Paul's Priory, Newport, RI.

6. Basil Pennington, "Prayer Makes Us Instruments of God's Peace," *Our Sunday Visitor,* January 5, 1992, 14.

S E V E N

1. Homer A. Watt and James B. Munn, *Ideas and Forms in English and American Literature* (New York: Scott Foresman and Co., 1925), 591.

2. Jaris Bragin, "Laughter Is the Best Medicine," *New Covenant,* January 1993.

3. Norman Cousins, *Head First: The Biology of Hope re: 10 years of scientific study on the healing power of the human spirit,* UCLA Medical School (New York: Villard, 1989) also *Anatomy of an Illness* (New York: W.W. Norton, 1979).

4. Dr. D. Cooper, cited by Bragin.

5. Cal Samra, "The Clown Therapy," *New Covenant,* November 1992. Also: Fellowship of Merry Christians, Cal Samra, Director, P.O. Box 895, Portage, MI 49081-0895.

6. Henri Nouwen, *The Return of the Prodigal Son* (New York: Doubleday, 1992).

7. Nouwen.

8. Dr. Ellen Sullens, "Happy or Sad, a Mood Can Prove Contagious," *New York Times,* October 5, 1991.

9. Etty Hillesum, *An Interrupted Life* (New York: Pantheon, 1991).

10. Fr. George DePrizio, "Are You Laughing with Me, Jesus?" (See Fellowship of Merry Christians, above).
11. Samra.
12. Annual directory, National Catholic Charismatic Service Committee, CHARICENTER, Box 628, Locust Grove, VA 22508, Phone: (703) 972-0225.

E I G H T

1. *Catechism of the Catholic Church*, English Translation, (Boston: Pauline, 1994), No. 2725.
2. Fr. Denis O'Brien, "The Garden," *All About Issues*, March/April 1992.
3. Documents of Vatican II, *On Revelation* (New York: Guild Press, America Press, Association Press, 1966), #257.
4. O'Brien, 36.
5. St. Teresa of Avila, *The Way of Perfection* (New York: Image, 1991), 22:71.
6. Peter Kreeft, "God and Me," *New Covenant*, July/August 1992, 22.
7. St. Thérèse of Lisieux, *The Story of a Soul* (Washington, D.C.: Inst. of Carmelite Studies).
8. Jean-Pierre de Caussade, *Abandonment to Divine Providence* (New York: Image, 1975), 78, 79.
9. Brent L. Bozell, "The Politics of Abandonment," *New Oxford Review*, January/February 1988.
10. Bernard Bangley, "The Practice of the Presence of God," *Spiritual Treasure, Paraphrases of the Spiritual Classics* (Mahwah, N.J.: Paulist, 1985), 67.
11. Joseph Hrdina, "Battling Cancer: The Gift Is in the Struggle," *Our Sunday Visitor*, January 6, 1992.

N I N E

1. Jim Manney, "Fainthearted Not!," *New Covenant,* April 1993, 3.
2. Fr. Thomas McDonnell, "That I May See," *The Pilot,* April 23, 1993, 14.
3. Dr. Sheila Cassidy, *Sharing the Darkness: The Spirituality of Caring* (Maryknoll, N.Y.: Orbis, 1991), 8.
4. Jean Vanier, "Seeing the Face of Jesus in the Face of the Poor," *The Word Among Us,* Gaithersburg, Va.
5. Sr. Jane Raphael Livingston, FSP, "When Love Is Difficult," *The Family,* July/August, 1992.
6. Pope John Paul II, address to elderly, Vancouver, Canada, June 1984.

T E N

1. Cardinal Joseph Bernardin, "My Friend Death," *Our Sunday Visitor,* December 1, 1996, 4.
2. Raniero Cantalamessa, OFM Cap., "In Love with Eternity," *New Covenant,* November 1992.
3. Cantalamessa.
4. Statement on Euthanasia, National Conference of Catholic Bishops, September 12, 1991.
5. Declaration on Euthanasia, The Ramsey Colloquium, Institute on Religion and Public Life, 156 5th Ave, N.Y., November 27, 1991.
6. Joseph R. Stanton, M.D., "Euthanasia," *Life Advocate,* October 1992.
7. Suicide polls, American Assn. of Suicidology, cited by Joseph Pisani, "Our Final Exit Should Be God's Decision," *Our Sunday Visitor,* December 1, 1991.

8. Center for Disease, cited by Pisani.

9. Joanne Lynn, M.D., Correspondence, *The New England Journal of Medicine*, 328, April 1, 1993, 964.

10. E. Joanne Angelo, M.D., "Transforming a Culture of Death into a Civilization of Love," Respect Life Program, Washington, D.C., NCCB Pro-Life Publications and Promotion, 1993.

11. Lillibeth Navarro, "The Doublespeak of 'Death With Dignity,'" *National Right to Life News*, March 30, 1993.

12. Kathy Coffey, "The Holiness of Death," *Our Sunday Visitor*, April 11, 1993.

13. George Gurtner, "Battling Cancer and Living on God's Time," *Our Sunday Visitor*, July 5, 1991.

14. Mitch Finley, interview with John Carmody, author of *Conversations with a Dying Friend* (Mahwah, N.J.: Paulist 1992), *Our Sunday Visitor*, March 28, 1993.

15. Declaration on Euthanasia, Congregation on the Doctrine of the Faith, Rome, May 5, 1980; also, Nutrition and Hydration: Moral and Pastoral Reflections, National Catholic Conference of Bishops, Secretariat for Pro-Life Activities, 3211 Fourth St., Washington, D.C. 20017.

16. Advance Directives for Health Care and Treatment, Pope John Center (for the Study of Ethics in Medicine) 186 Forbes Rd., Braintree, MA 02184 ; also Self-Protection Document, Dr. Joseph Stanton, Value of Life Committee, Mass. Citizens for Life, 529 Main St., Boston, MA 02129. Both give information on a Durable Power of Attorney or Health Care Proxy.

17. Fr. Thomas McDonnell, "Christ's Agony in the Garden," *The Pilot*, March 12, 1993, 14.

THE HEALING POWER OF HOPE

The
Healing Power
of Hope

Down-to-Earth Alternatives
to Euthanasia
and Assisted Suicide

MARY DRAHOS
FOREWORD BY DR. JOSEPH R. STANTON, M.D.

CHARIS

SERVANT PUBLICATIONS
ANN ARBOR, MICHIGAN

Charis Books is an imprint of Servant Publications especially designed to serve
Roman Catholics.

Scripture texts used in this work are taken from the Revised Standard Version of the
Bible, © 1946, 1952, 1971 by the Division of Christian Education of the National
Council of Churches of Christ in the USA. Used by permission.

Although the stories in this book are true, names have been changed to protect the
privacy of those involved.

Published by Servant Publications
P.O. Box 8617
Ann Arbor, Michigan 48107

Cover photo: Tony Vassel

97 98 99 00 01 10 9 8 7 6 5 4 3 2 1

Printed in the United States of America
ISBN 1-56955-030-1

LIBRARY OF CONGRESS CATALOGING-IN-PUBLICATION DATA

Drahos, Mary.
The healing power of hope : down to earth alternatives to euthanasia and assisted
suicide / Mary Drahos : foreword by Joseph R. Stanton.
    p.   cm.
Includes bibliographical references.
ISBN 1-56955-030-1
1. Suffering—Religious aspects—Christianity.   2. Hope—Religious aspects—
Christianity.   3. Terminally ill—Religious life.   4. Church work with the terminally
ill—Catholic Church.   5. Euthanasia—Religious aspects—Christianity—
Controversial literature.   6. Assisted suicide—Religious aspects—Christianity—
Controversial literature.   7. Catholic Church—Doctrines.   I. Title.
BT732.7.D73   1997
248.8'6—dc21   97-3388
                                                                                    CIP